GOD
WRESTLING

Books by

Mike Evans

FROM BETHANY HOUSE PUBLISHERS

The Unanswered Prayers of Jesus

God-Wrestling

GOD
WRESTLING

LIKE JACOB *of* OLD,
A LIFE-CHANGING ENCOUNTER
with the ALMIGHTY

MIKE EVANS

BETHANY HOUSE PUBLISHERS
Minneapolis, Minnesota

God-Wrestling
Copyright © 2004
Mike Evans

Cover design by David Carlson

Published by Bethany House Publishers
11400 Hampshire Avenue South
Bloomington, Minnesota 55438
www.bethanyhouse.com

Bethany House Publishers is a Division of
Baker Book House Company, Grand Rapids, Michigan.

Printed in the United States of America

Library of Congress Cataloging-in-Publication Data

Evans, Mike, 1947-
   God-wrestling : like Jacob of old, a life-changing encounter with the Almighty / by Mike Evans.
   p. cm.
   ISBN 0-7642-2758-0 (pbk.)
   1. Christian life. 2. Religious awakening--Christianity. I. title.

BV4509.5.E837 2004
248.4--dc22

                                   2003022371

Dedication

This book is dedicated to the local pastors, the guardians of the most powerful force on earth. They have given what they could not keep to gain what they could not lose. These men and women of God are the true hope for a great awakening . . . the proclaimers of truth . . . and have maintained moral clarity in a world gone mad.

One of America's greatest presidents, Ronald Reagan, told me in the Oval Office, "The greatest force in America is not the Republican or Democratic Party. They only meet once every four years. The greatest force in America is the church; they meet weekly. They are a spiritual organization, committed to traditional family values . . . the glue that holds our great nation together."

About the Author

Mike Evans is one of the most informed, inspirational, and sought-after speakers in the world. He is a *New York Times* and *Time* magazine best-selling author, and a confidant to world leaders. Millions throughout the world have seen the prime-time specials he has hosted; these programs have received national awards on thirteen different occasions. Guests have included: Kathie Lee Gifford, Evander Holyfield, Deion Sanders, Steve Allen, Gavin MacLeod, James Garner, Pat Boone, Monty Hall, and Jayne Meadows.

Evans has been published in the *Wall Street Journal,* the *Jerusalem Post, Newsweek,* and hundreds of publications throughout the world. He is an award-winning journalist, a member of the National Press Club, and has covered world events for more than two decades. He has appeared on hundreds of radio and television broadcasts, including *Good Morning America; Nightline; Crossfire;* and *The Good Morning Show* (Great Britain); and is a frequent guest on the FOX Network. He has appeared on NBC, ABC, CBS, and CNN World News.

As a public speaker, Evans has addressed more than four thousand audiences throughout the world. In the United States, he has spoken at the Orange Bowl, Giants Stadium, and Arrowhead Stadium. In the last decade alone, he spoke to more than ten million people. Six hundred thousand people have come to Christ around the globe through his meetings. More than 110,000 ministers have attended his pastors' schools. Mr. Evans is a specialist in assisting pastors in strategic planning, life management goals, and how to impact their cities.

Evans' wife, Carolyn, is Chairwoman and Founder of the Christian Woman of the Year Association. Ruth Bell Graham, Elizabeth Dole, and Mother Teresa are among the recipients who have been honored over the past fifteen years. The Executive Committee is comprised of a number of prominent women, including Dr. Cory SerVaas, owner of the *Saturday Evening Post.*

Contents

CHAPTER ONE

The Kiss of God

And Jacob was left alone; and there wrestled a man with him
until the breaking of the day. And . . . [the man] touched
the hollow of his thigh.
GENESIS 32:24–25

We *need Jesus.* We sing about how much we need Jesus. We
pray, "Jesus help me, I need you." We've felt the arms of our Savior, heard Him speak to our hearts, and believed that we have
been with Him. We've experienced His salvation, grace, forgiveness, and mercy. Sometimes we've seen His miracles or experienced His life bursting through our own.

Despite how we've felt, the miracles we've heard reported, the
success we've seen on the mission fields, and the "revivals" breaking out all around us, today a growing number of Christians
intensely yearn to be with Jesus more than ever before. For us, it's
no longer enough to attain a spiritual high at a service, if we then

go back to living a "sincere Christian life," blessing His name through music and prayer while the hordes of hell daily rob us.

I've experienced what I can only describe as "the kiss of God" in my life—events that were so spectacular I could never understand why they happened . . . until now. They always came when I had the least amount of confidence in myself, and it seemed that God had intentionally exhausted me. *In fact, that's exactly what needed to happen so I would learn to trust Him.*

> *I've experienced what I can only describe as "the kiss of God" in my life—events that were so spectacular I could never understand why they happened . . . until now.*

The vibrant relationship we have with Christ is far more than the scheduled services, prayer meetings, and brief quiet times! Jesus has always been Jesus, all the time. *Almost every miracle Jesus performed was an interruption in His schedule.* He yearns to interrupt our earthly schedule to be with us and be duplicated in our lives so we will do greater things *with* Him. His ministry is the kiss I've experienced.

Divine Disappointments

"Hold your head straight, Mr. Evans," the optometrist said as he examined my eyes. The more I tried, the more difficult it became. I realized my head was shaking uncontrollably because of neck tremors. Finally, the optometrist said, "Mr. Evans, you need to go to a neurologist to find out what is wrong with your neck."

That admonition began eight years of trudging from one specialist to another. I must have seen more than one hundred neurologists, orthopedic specialists, and others in an attempt to determine the source of the muscle spasms in my neck and resulting head tremors. Little did I know that I had a strange neurological ailment called spasmodic *tortocollis destonia*—a rare genetic disease.

The harder I tried to hold my head straight, the more difficult it became. The muscles pulled my neck and twisted my head. The only way I could hold my head erect was to press my chin down with my hand.

As months and years passed, it grew worse and worse. At first, I tried denial, assuming it would get better after a few weeks. When that did not happen, depression followed as I realized the disease could result in total disability. It was, at the very least, humiliating, especially for a public speaker.

No matter what I did, tremors were my constant companion. I was told that I must have an emotional problem, or perhaps was headed for a breakdown. Instead of reaching out for support, I attempted to fake it. In time, I developed tachycardia. In seconds, my heart would jump from 80 to 120 beats per minute, and would race for 10 to 20 minutes. I felt as if I was dying.

This led to panic attacks that would grip me at the most inopportune times. I was preaching in as many as twelve different churches. While in the pulpit, a panic attack would hit like an electrical shock. It was humiliating and depressing. I became so discouraged that I stopped preaching for fourteen months. I was thirty-two years old, and it looked like my ministry was over.

The more I looked in the mirror, the more distressed I became. I questioned why I couldn't be strong like other preachers. Little did I know that God wasn't asking me to be strong, He was asking me to allow Him to be the strength of my life. The more I thought about it, the more depressed I became. Ultimately, I realized I needed to turn the entire situation over to Jesus. I got on my face in prayer and sobbed as I poured my heart out to God. I prayed, "Lord, I look around and I'm distressed. I look within and I'm depressed. But I am going to look to Jesus and be at rest."

Like David of old, I stood on the Word of God: "The Lord is the strength of my life, of whom shall I be afraid?" (Psalm 27:1).

"Even though I walk through the valley of the shadow of death, I will fear no evil, for you are with me" (Psalm 23:4 NIV).

"I sought the LORD, and he answered me; he delivered me from all my fears" (Psalm 34:4 NIV).

"You will not fear the terror of night, nor the arrow that flies by day . . ." (Psalm 91:3 NIV).

"For God hath not given us the spirit of fear; but of power, and of love, and of a sound mind" (2 Timothy 1:7).

The reality is this: During that period of time, I produced more award-winning specials and wrote more books than at any other time in my life. As a matter of fact, it seemed that supernatural doors were opening for me to be a confidant to world leaders more than at any other time in my life.

I truly understood what it meant to know Christ "in the fellowship of His suffering, and in the power of His resurrection" (Philippians 3:10). I had to reach out to Christ to complete me in areas that were lacking. He made me to become what I was not.

Doctors suggested that I find a support group to help me deal with an incurable disease. I was told I would be that way all of my life. The only "support group" I attended was daily prayer with the Father, Son, and Holy Spirit. (I am not opposed to support groups, but I could not accept the fact that I would be disabled for the rest of my life.)

Eight years after the first diagnosis, I underwent eight and a half hours of surgery by one of the doctors who initially discovered the gene. The surgery completely stopped the neck spasms.

Approximately eight weeks after the surgery, I was in Saudi Arabia and Iraq during the Persian Gulf War to proclaim the Gospel of Jesus Christ. As Paul said, "When I am weak, then I am strong" (2 Corinthians 12:10).

How Little, How Rare

The great embarrassment I now face is that the remarkable part of these stories is not how marvelously or how often God has manifested himself through me, but rather how little He does and how rare are those precious times. I have hindered *Him,* too self-centered to understand that He was not blessing "me and my ministry" but allowing me to take part in *His* ministry. I assumed that I had a gift of the Holy Spirit empowering me, when the truth is that the person of Jesus Christ had simply found a way to work through me to glorify the Father.

Because we are Christians, we rarely dream we could be the problem. At that time, in my mind, the only problem was the devil. I've never wept as much as I have in realizing the shameful truth. Jesus already defeated the devil. Now His greatest problem in manifesting His ministry in my life is *me.* My heart's desire, by the grace of God, is to live my remaining years not allowing my self to take over the throne of my life, where Jesus needs to be Lord and King.

> *Because we are Christians, we rarely dream we could be the problem.*

It's all about Jesus—walking, talking, touching, and fully manifesting himself on earth—until even the shadows of ordinary believers are transformed, through the power of the Holy Spirit, into the shadow of Jesus. This is not pie-in-the-sky theology. This is precisely what God will do in the greatest awakening the world has ever seen, which will usher in the return of the Lord Jesus Christ and gather the final harvest. The apostle Paul declared:

> [I pray that] the eyes of your understanding [are] being enlightened; that ye may know what is the hope of His calling, and what [are] the riches of the glory of His inheritance in the saints, and what is the exceeding greatness of His power toward us who believe, according to the working of His mighty power. . . . Till we all come in the unity of the faith and of the knowledge of the Son of God, unto a perfect man, unto the measure of the stature of the fullness of Christ. (Ephesians 1:18–19; 4:13)

A perfect man! *There is only one: Jesus.* Attaining the measure of the stature of the fullness of Christ is not about preaching or singing, although these have a part. It's not about programs or plans. It's not even about ministries. *It's about Jesus*—all His glory and all His riches and all His majesty—manifesting himself as He chooses, where He chooses, and when He chooses, *through us.* I want to know Jesus as the disciples did, as the early church did. We want to reach out with a healing touch to those around us . . . but *how can we do it?*

Stop the Roller Coaster!

Two thousand years ago, during the Jewish feast of Pentecost, God poured out His Spirit upon the earth in such a powerful manifestation that it changed the world. Christ's ministry has continued since then as a present-day ministry through the lives of ordinary believers.

On the Day of Pentecost, Peter experienced a complete transformation. This man, who had been on a Christian roller-coaster ride—believing one day, denying the next—suddenly stood up and spoke out, prophetically and boldly. Three thousand people were added to the kingdom of God that day.

Peter became a God-wrestler. He'd started out just like us. He knew Jesus. He experienced the love of Jesus. He believed on Jesus and named Him as the Messiah. He personally experienced miracles (such as when he walked on the water). Peter received full forgiveness and grace after Jesus rose from the dead and appeared to him. Jesus blessed him; Peter ate and had fellowship with the Lord. Jesus took time to disciple Peter, taking a personal interest in him.

All of this was still not enough. Peter made futile attempts at "living a Christian life," but it was (and *is*) impossible to do. No matter what he did, Peter was still Peter, trying to prevail with God in his own strength. His name alone did not qualify him to experience divine visitation. He was humiliated that he couldn't live up to the victorious Christian life taught by his Teacher. Then he denied the Savior and felt like an outcast among the disciples. He was embarrassed to show himself in the city where people knew who he was. However, on the Day of Pentecost, something happened in Peter that was personally earth-shaking, and, through him and the other disciples, it shook the entire world.

Peter had seen Jesus after His resurrection. Peter had known that Jesus was alive. *But on the Day of Pentecost, Peter discovered Jesus was alive in him!*

This was more than an "infilling" with the Holy Spirit and power, more than a spiritual high that made him resolve to live his life in a better way. Peter was changed! This same Peter (with John) later went into the city and saw a man begging. *"Look on us,"* he said.

Why did he draw attention to himself? Peter *had been* ashamed to show his face. What was there to see in him? *Now* Peter knew that if the man looked, he would see Jesus in him: Peter had become Christ's representation, fulfilling His mission and ministry on earth. What was so different? Peter had been with Jesus, and the life of Jesus was in Peter to glorify the Father.

Nothing is more important to God today than to manifest His Son fully and completely in the life of the believer; for this He is ready to move all of heaven and earth.

Jesus has a present-day ministry. He is no longer physically here, but His ministry continues in the lives of believers, just as if He were. Christ, living in us and through us, can continue His mission on earth.

Christians today are being called to manifest nothing less than the present-day ministry of Christ: Jesus manifesting himself fully and completely through us, unhindered, in the person of the Holy Spirit, so He can fulfill His purposes on a daily, hourly, and moment-by-moment basis. Jesus fulfilled His present-day ministry through the early church in the lives of Peter and other believers, and those God-wrestlers turned the world upside down!

> *Nothing is more important to God today than to manifest His Son fully and completely in the life of the believer.*

Jesus told His disciples they would see greater things than what He had already done. We are yearning to see this today. We want to see His prophecies fulfilled and His prayers answered. We want the visitation of Jesus the disciples had. When Paul's clothes were sent to the sick, the sick recovered. People ran, chasing the shadow of Peter, because if even his shadow touched them they would be healed. *That's revival!*

Jesus Gave Us His Ministry Unhindered

I've seen and experienced the unhindered work of Christ. How and why it happened, I did not understand until I went further into prayer than I had ever gone. That's where I discovered these truths.

I am the least likely qualified to bring them to you. I grew up in an abusive home. Because of my mother's heritage and teaching, I was brutalized by a "Christian" father. At age four, I started running away. I remember the police once bringing me back . . . and I was quickly locked in the canning closet for punishment. *There I prayed my first prayer with a broken, hungry heart.*

At age six, I was a stuttering, dysfunctional, and wrecked little boy. Yet, inexplicably, I remember the date of an important decision I made that year. On September 12, while playing in a park in the early evening, a group from the nearby nursing home came out to feed the pigeons. With tubes and bottles dangling around their wheelchairs, they held pieces of bread in their shriveled hands and threw them about. They offered some to me, but I threw the bread down and ran home, crying, "I don't want to feed the pigeons!" Without conscious awareness, I had a divine discontentment that shrank at the thought of living my whole life without any sense of meaning, simply inhaling and exhaling and ending up in some park feeding the birds.

Those precious people, in my mind's eye, are symbolic of Christians we've seen grow old around us. How heartbreaking to think we could end up with only birdfeed to show for our lives. I see that devastated little boy as symbolic of what many of us *are* spiritually. Stuttering in our efforts, dysfunctional in our relationships, illiterate in the things of God; yet unwilling to remain that way, we stumble through life.

We have to realize that if we continue to do what we've done in the past, in the future we'll have only what we've always had. *I don't want that for my life.* I understand that it's time to wrestle with God because I want His fire to consume me. I want Jesus to live in all His glory through me, to speak through me, to love through me, and to reach through me. It's not about *me;* it's about *Him*! It's about the King of Kings and Lord of Lords having full lordship in my life and yours.

It wasn't until Jesus appeared to this little boy (at age eleven) that a ray of God's light entered my life. It was my first experience of intimacy with Jesus, even though I didn't know what that fully meant until recently. After a stint in the military, determined to live for Him, I went to a Bible college. Anything I knew about Christians had come from my Catholic community in Massachusetts. I'll never forget asking when I arrived at the Bible school, "Where do we pick up our robes?"

At age nineteen, I began preaching the gospel. For thirty-two years I worked as hard as I possibly could to reach the lost, from the marble halls of the U.S. government to the hellholes of the world. When I felt the kiss of God, I thought He was blessing my ministry. *I didn't understand He was actually blessing His.*

In addition, I saw it inconsistently. I sometimes experienced the supernatural, but I couldn't maintain supernatural living. I never dreamed that God wants to kiss us even more than we want to be kissed.

The gospel of Luke describes a sinful woman who brought an alabaster box of ointment to anoint Jesus as He visited the home of a Pharisee named Simon. The woman wept and washed His feet with her tears while wiping them with her hair, kissing His feet and anointing them with oil. Some rebuked her, but Jesus said, "You did not give me a kiss, but this woman, from the time I entered, has not stopped kissing my feet. You did not put oil on my head, but she has poured perfume on my feet" (7:45–46 NIV).

The same Christ is reaching out to us today. *Hers is the spirit that turns God's head and moves God's hand—the spirit of humility and brokenness.*

What *Is* the Problem?

We are hindered when self instead of Christ is on the throne of our lives. This is why the divorce rate in the church is rising, keeping up with and sometimes outpacing that of society. This is why church kids turn to cults, gangs, and drugs. *We try sincerely, but we don't seem to realize we are sincerely trying to live the Christian life in our own strength.* In so doing, we retain our self—our own interests and concerns—as the center of our identity. Yes, we strive to be good Christians, but who really gets the final word when the pressure is on? Is it Christ in us, or just us?

Although I continued struggling for more than three decades to be the best possible father, husband, and Christian, I failed. I failed because I was attempting to live up to a standard I could never achieve. No one can. Only Christ can live that standard, and He lives it *through us.* When He does, we know the meaning of the measure of the stature of the fullness of Christ, and we see God's glorious promises manifested in our lives. Then the world knows that we have been with Jesus.

We cannot win in the natural what Christ has won at Calvary. All attempts to do so are paramount to treason. *In essence, when we claim to be able to live the Christ life ourselves, without Him on the throne of our lives, we attempt to compete with the blood He shed on the cross.* Instead of a great awakening, we will experience a rude awakening if we don't repent!

Until our hearts are fully and completely surrendered to the Lord, self will only put Band-Aids on festering sores. The wonderful reality is that Christ has already won the battle. *When you and I realize it's about "Him" and not about "you" or "me," God will reign triumphant in our lives. Hallelujah!*

CHAPTER TWO

It's All About Jesus

*Now thanks be to God who always leads us in triumph in Christ,
and through us diffuses the fragrance of His knowledge in every
place. For we are to God the fragrance of Christ.*
2 CORINTHIANS 2:14–15 NKJV

Christ's prayer "Your will be done on earth as it is in heaven"
(Matthew 6:10) shows His desire for the Father's will to be freely
accomplished here—*unhindered*—as in heaven. Why, then, is
there such a barrier to even *His* prayers being fulfilled?

In the early 1970s, while in the military, I was stationed at
Wong Tong Nee, Korea, where I visited Dr. Paul Cho's (compar-
atively small) "Revival Center at Sodaemoon," as it was then
called. Now their members number over 750,000! Back then I
saw about two thousand people praying, rocking back and forth
and crying out to the Lord. They were so caught up and so
impassioned for Christ that their pursuit of the presence of God

humbled me. Over two decades later when I visited again, they were still praying with passion. On that trip, Dr. Cho taught me a painful lesson as we sat together in a restaurant in downtown Seoul.

"Tell me, Pastor Cho," I said earnestly, leaning across the table toward him. "What is the number one key to having an effective ministry across the globe?"

"Brother," he said in his beautifully accented English, "you must understand that you cannot help Jesus Christ, but you can hinder Him. Jesus sees your ministry. He wants to show you His."

I returned to my hotel room with my gears stripped. *I can't help Jesus? But I thought I was one of the good guys who helped Him! Isn't it Satan who hinders Jesus?* I have begun to understand what Dr. Cho knew: Although we ask God to remove the barriers to our prayers, self is the biggest hindrance.

We pray for more power and more faith, but many times don't realize we are asking God to empower our flesh. The apostle Paul taught that the kingdom of God is not things of the flesh, but righteousness, peace, and joy in the Holy Spirit (see Romans 14:17). It's time to stop asking God to bless what our flesh is doing and to start blessing what He's doing. A lot of what we're doing is a

> *We pray for more power and more faith, but many times don't realize we are asking God to empower our flesh.*

mess, and God won't bless our mess! It's not what we're doing that brings God's blessing, but finding out what Jesus is doing and blessing His work.

We rebuke the devil, but the majority of what we think are his attacks are actually self-inflicted wounds from disobedience. When we try to use religious pride to enter what we believe is the presence of God, we only become judgmental and arrogant, feeling comfortable in gossiping about others because we think we "know."

The devil cannot stop the present-day ministry of Jesus Christ: "For this purpose the Son of God was manifested, that He might destroy the works of the devil" (1 John 3:8). The only thing Satan can do is manipulate who or what will exert lordship over our lives. Satan wants to exalt flesh, which is self. Self wants identity. Self wants to trust self. Self wants control, and self is intoxicated by the seduction of power. The biggest lord we've served, the biggest obstacle to Christ's ministry, is self.

People talk about Jesus, but demons will tremble only when they see His ministry manifested. *It's all about being with Jesus.* When we've been with Jesus, we're blessed in His presence. "[Jacob] said [to the man], 'I will not let thee go, except thou bless me'" (Genesis 32:26). Do you have this passion for God?

The power of the Holy Spirit, the coming great awakening, the present-day ministry of Jesus Christ, and the glory that will cover the earth—all are barred by the same obstacle: self.

What exactly can we do, if we can't help Jesus?

What does Jesus need? He needs believers who will not hinder Him so His final mission on earth can be completed. People who have been with Christ are the most important item on His calendar.

When we press into Jesus, we burst through the loins of the Lion of Judah as men and women of destiny, filled with holy fire and transforming everything we touch. When we fully comprehend what it means to be with Jesus, our lives are changed forever.

What a life to aspire to!

If you have been with Jesus, the life of Jesus will be manifested in you and through you. God is ready to move heaven and earth to accomplish His purposes for the man or woman who has been with Jesus.

Others know when you've been with Jesus. God is raising up a people who will spend time with Him, who are determined to do everything in their power to release Christ to fulfill His destiny through them and impact a lost and dying world.

Something Is Wrong With This Picture

How could Jesus have prayed or prophesied what seems like wishful thinking, pie-in-the-sky dreaming? Rarely does an average churchgoer have the ambition to do greater things than Christ did. We generally wrestle to obey His Spirit within us rather than wrestling and pressing forward to fulfill the promise that even greater works would be accomplished.

Churches struggle just to fill Sunday services and teach members to tithe 10 percent. In no way has the church taken over the world, as Christ intended when He called us the *ekklesia* (Greek for "ruling body"). If Christ has delegated His power to each believer, there is truly something wrong with the picture today!

The spirit of competition, fueled by flesh, fills the body with boasts: "First Church [ours] is bigger than Second Church"; "We have a better choir"; "We have a larger budget"; and "We have stronger programs." Sister Smith is on the phone gossiping all day about everything that he said or she said about anyone in the church, and then ends it with "I'm just telling you so you can pray." *Let's get to the place where we finally cut off our flesh!*

We claim to be baptized with the Holy Spirit, but we know nothing about fire. John the Baptist said we would be baptized with the Holy Spirit *and* fire; this fire burns up the flesh, even "religious" flesh.

We have the Holy Spirit, but does the Holy Spirit have us? So many of us say, "I have Jesus." Perhaps the real question is *"Does Jesus have me—all of me?"*

It's time we do what we've signed up to do: empty ourselves, allowing God to fill us with His fire. We can't fellowship with Jesus without experiencing the fire of God. So many declare, "I am the righteousness of Christ." Well, what part of us is the righteousness of Christ? It isn't our works, our deeds, our acts, and it certainly isn't us! The only righteousness is Christ *in* us, shining and working *through* us when we surrender. The scandal of the cross is that Christ is right and righteous—and we are not.

Jesus drove a nail through all the works of the flesh.

Humankind, in a battle between the flesh and the purposes of God, crucified Christ out of a determination to be righteous in the flesh. Religion tries everything—including man-made rules, legalistic standards, and the doctrines of men—to improve or domesticate the flesh. Religions try to convince us we are holy by what we *do:*

Holy because we go to church

Holy because we read the Bible

Holy because we pray

Holy because we dress a certain way

Holy because we don't do certain things

Not true. *Jesus is the One who is holy.* Only when Christ in all of His glory is abiding in us are we also holy. We say *others* are in the flesh, but certainly not *us.* The truth is, we can be sincere but be sincerely *wrong,* wallowing in the flesh and not even knowing it. The flesh does not fear God because the flesh does not live in the light of eternity. When we understand that *we* live our lives in the light of eternity, *then* we will fear the Lord.

What a tragedy that Christians can have a Bible under their arm, don a choir robe, hold a communion cup in their hand, have a Sunday school pin for perfect attendance on their lapel, and say, "Lord, I've cast out demons in your name and I've healed the sick," yet hear these words: "Depart from me, you cursed worker of iniquity . . . I never knew you."

It's all about Jesus. He has no predecessor and no successor. The grave couldn't hold Him. There was no one before Him, and no one will come after Him. We can't live without Him, and we can't live outside of Him.

We can only expose self, our greatest hindrance to fellowship with Him, and take it to the cross so He can manifest himself in our lives. *We need all of Him—the living Christ—in all His glory!*

Reign With Christ Through the Storms

I've been with this personal Jesus. At age eleven, after witnessing another Friday night beating of my mother, I sneaked into my bedroom and sat on the edge of my bed, crying with my head in my hands. Suddenly I could see light around my hands, and I cringed, thinking my father had come into the room to beat me, too. Instead, as I moved my fingers to peek, I saw glowing, nail-scarred hands reaching toward me. Stunning! I followed them up to the smiling face of a Man lighting up the whole room. *I've never seen eyes so beautiful.* All the colors of the rainbow were in those eyes. I could see eternity through those eyes. They were smiling eyes. *It was Jesus!*

He said three important things to that little boy. The first was *"Son,"* the term I'd never been called before, the name that now gave me a sense of belonging I'd never had. The second was *"I love you."* I loved my mother, a precious woman who was abused first by her father and then by her husband, but I don't recall ever hearing her say, "I love you." Like most abused children, I assumed I was unlovable—but now the radiant Christ had said He loved me! Lastly: *"I have a wonderful plan for your life."*

I didn't know who He was, but I believed in Him. I didn't believe in healing, because my father had mocked Oral Roberts (seen on television) and told me healing was fake. Yet in that moment I was divinely healed of my stuttering and ulcers. I didn't know what "deliverance" meant, but I was miraculously and instantaneously delivered from fear. I didn't know what a "sinner's prayer" was, but I was gloriously converted. All because I had been with Jesus!

You will never reign with Christ in the sunshine if you refuse to allow Christ to reign through you in the storms.

Anxious to serve Him, I tried for many years to be a great evangelist. People applauded me. I served on prestigious committees. I had the esteem and favor of men, but I didn't walk in God's grace or peace. I called the ministry "my burden."

When I turned thirty-two, everything I'd worked so hard to achieve came crashing down. I was working nonstop, sixteen hours a day, seven days a week, thinking I had to keep up the pace for Jesus. I ended up in a cardiac ward with stress-induced constricted arteries and a rare neurological disease. I didn't dare tell anyone for fear they wouldn't have me in their churches or conferences again.

> *When self stubbornly refuses to give up control, your heart is incapable of being broken by what breaks the heart of God.*

When self stubbornly refuses to give up control, your heart is incapable of being broken by what breaks the heart of God.

Finally, in desperation, I called Jamie Buckingham from the hospital: "I'm afraid; please don't tell anyone about this." His comforting words were, "I'd be afraid, too."

When I hung up the phone, I raised my hands and said, "Lord, I'm sick, I'm tired, and I'm not going to lower these hands until you show up, Jesus, and touch me as you did when I was eleven." It had been so long. After what seemed like an eternity, God bathed me with the sweet love, grace, and peace I'd longed for but repeatedly missed.

From another room in that hospital ward, I could hear a man crying out, "God, help me! God, help me!" Jesus spoke softly to me, and I pulled off all the hospital wires, alerting the nurses to come running. They allowed me a brief visit to the man's room. I asked him if he was scared, told him I was, too, and then laid my hands on him and began to pray.

My problem wasn't physical. It was spiritual. I had tried to live my Christian life in my own strength and found that I couldn't. No one told me that ministers could be afraid or have insecurities, so I'd hidden mine. Even so, they weren't hidden from God, or myself, and eventually they overcame me. What I didn't understand is that having the fellowship and suffering of Christ in my life means being willing to admit everything that I'm not. I was afraid to admit what I wasn't for fear of rejection, but when I did, Christ revealed to me who He was, and then I understood the apostle Paul when he said,

[I count all my "credentials" as loss] that I may know him, and the power of his resurrection, and the fellowship of his sufferings. (Philippians 3:8, 10)

The fellowship of His sufferings is acknowledging what we're not. God doesn't leave us there. He takes what we're not and infuses us with what He *is*. The power of the Resurrection is Christ manifested in all of His glory.

We are human beings in need of a Holy Spirit dose of humility so we can first acknowledge what we're not. When we do, Christ acknowledges who He is and fuses the two together. When what we're *not* and what God *is* come together, we experience Jesus in the power of His resurrection, and His present-day ministry can be manifested in all His glory, in us and through us.

What We're Not Fuses With What God Is

The entire battle is over the present-day ministry of Jesus. How does His ministry fully function between you and your spouse, you and your children, you and your job, you and your other relationships? Many sincere believers try hard to die to the flesh by remembering, "What would Jesus do?" But it's not what we think He would do that shakes hell. *It's Satan seeing what He has done—in us!* We have to surrender our kingdom to the King of Kings and the Lord of Lords, letting Jesus do what He wants to do through our lives.

From the time I ended up in that cardiac ward, I was struggling. *Why?* I kept asking God. I wept intermittently for more than fourteen months, often sitting on the back steps of our ministry offices. All the pain and hurt I had experienced as a child resurfaced in my emotions. Instead of seeing the loving faces of those around me, I only saw my father's face—laughing at me and telling me what a failure I was. I felt that I was failing and dying inside. What I didn't realize was that I *had* to die: die to my flesh and my pride. I'd lived the Christ-ian life, but not the Christ life.

God's glory wants to blast like a fire through our being, drawing us into such fellowship with Jesus that we will know that we know that we know we have been with Him; those around us will know the same. Without total commitment, our self life is both an instrument of Satan and the greatest hindrance to the glory of God being manifested in and through us on earth.

It's Me in Christ!

Many of us want to say we've been with Jesus, but we're all in the same boat: we can't get there. Something is holding us back. We frequently go through the week mechanically, reacting first and praying second. We can't seem to get the two reversed!

Christians have tried to live the Christian life and failed. We've not taken over the world; the world has taken over us. The popular phrase "Christ in me" has created a theology where essentially we say, "I want to use faith, I want to use prayer; I want to use my Christian culture so I can be everything possible, based upon the limited understanding I have." This thinking will always lead to defeat.

It's me hid away in Christ! It's Him living in me, and my self dying. We must not be confused by our own clichés.

Some years ago, in Orlando, I awakened early to catch a flight to Michigan. As soon as I got settled on the plane, I fell asleep. Hours later, in a daze, I heard the pilot saying, "We're now over Phoenix, Arizona." I was totally confused. I asked the attendant, "How can we possibly be over Phoenix? We're going to Michigan."

"This plane is not bound for Michigan," she replied. "We're going to Los Angeles."

I was so frustrated. Then I heard Jesus gently instruct me to pray. As I did, He said I was going as a witness for Him to Los Angeles. At the L.A. airport, I didn't sense an open door to witness to anyone. Frustrated again, I found a seat to wait for the only flight out, which was to Ohio. A woman wearing a maternity dress sat across from me in the waiting area, so I figured I might as well witness to her. I began, "When is your baby due?" She stood up and cursed me out loud. She wasn't pregnant—just heavy.

By the time I boarded the plane, I was fed up, so I just took a pillow and ignored the man next to me. He talked anyway. Finally, I opened my eyes and he said, "You must be somebody."

Christians have tried to live the Christian life and failed. We've not taken over the world; the world has taken over us.

"A somebody who thinks he's a somebody is a nobody," I answered, "but a nobody who experiences a Somebody becomes a somebody. As long as a somebody thinks he's a somebody, he will always be a nobody."

"What are you talking about?" he said. Instantly Jesus whispered to me, *That's the man.* The person of the Holy Spirit gave me a word about his life, regarding a past divorce and tremendous personal problems. It was as if I had opened his mail. The color drained from his face.

"Who are you?" he demanded. "You frighten me." He thought I was a government agent who had some kind of inside scoop.

We ended up talking for a couple of hours, and I led him to the Lord. When the plane landed, I discovered that sitting behind me was the governor of Ohio, and in front of me was Pete Rose, the former baseball player. As we waited to deplane, Pete mused, "Well, you kept *me* awake most of the flight!"

"Pete," I said, "Christ loves you. Someday you're going to get on a plane called 'Flight Final.' When you arrive at your destination, there will only be One cheering for you. If His precious blood has washed your sins away, you'll step into the largest stadium full of cheering heavenly angels and saints [you have ever seen], but if it hasn't, you'll step into an eternity of darkness."

The Lord Jesus Christ had an appointment, and He took me

with Him. *In life, it is either Christ in me, the hope of glory, or me in me, hoping for glory.*

The enemy is raging because he sees the imminence of the great visitation. He wants to turn God's children away from the mighty sea of deliverance, but Jesus is praying for us, and God is sending His angels to strengthen us. When the final storm hits, without God's glory in the lives of believers who have been with Jesus, we would be devastated by darkness.

Beloved, the Father knows your troubled heartaches. *Let Him kiss you with His Son.* Then the King will truly live in your lives. Unfortunately, many of us live as though He is not King of the present but King only of the past.

From the time I was eleven, I knew how to get "low" with Jesus. I would humble myself before God and experience His power, but in three to six months, I'd be burdened again. I couldn't get out of the cycle. Then I'd become desperate, humble myself before God again, and He would do the supernatural, continuing the cycle. I didn't get it!

We don't seem to get it as believers today. We do not allow Christ's Spirit full access to our lives. We allow the Christ-ian life to become our burden instead of allowing Christ to live His life through us unhindered. We have engraved His name, reputation, and authority on everything but our hearts.

We must not be content to sit in the bleachers idolizing "stars" rather than having our flesh buried so that the world can behold Jesus, the Bright and Morning Star, through us.

CHAPTER THREE

"Sir, We Would See Jesus"

We know that, when he [Jesus] shall appear, we shall be like him;
for we shall see him as he is.
1 JOHN 3:2

We will never be able to see anything eternal without a Holy Spirit-led prayer life. The Bible says the heart is deceitfully wicked; *who could know it?* The present-day ministry of Jesus Christ will be manifested and released on this earth, but not on our terms, no matter how sincere or religious we are.

The eyes of God, the spotlight of heaven, search for hungry hearts willing to surrender to the person of the Holy Spirit, thirsting to be with Jesus.

Christ has determined that we will rule and reign with Him. It's His mission—not only when we get to heaven, but also on earth.

Satan Has Goals for You

Satan's two greatest goals are (1) to convince you to live the Christian life yourself, in your own strength, and (2) to make you believe that you must be "worthy" and "righteous." With these ungodly goals achieved, disillusioned Christians continue to leave the church in droves.

Why do the unsaved resist the gospel? Because they say, "I can't live it." Why do they say this? They're right. They see us trying and failing to live the Christian life in our own religious flesh.

> *When we allow Christ to live through us, the world will run to Jesus!*

When we allow Christ to live through us, the world will run to Jesus!

If Christianity were not about being with Jesus, then what would it be about? What would be the point or purpose? When the church is not about being with Jesus, it has no divine purpose or mission to influence a lost and dying world. These goals separate us from the Power Source that will crush Satan's head.

Christ can quench all the fiery darts of the enemy, no matter what the circumstances. With *self* in charge, we feebly attempt to contact God flesh-to-Spirit. With *Jesus* on the throne of our lives, we experience spirit-to-Spirit contact. The same Holy Spirit of God from Pentecost is available to each and every believer today.

When we fear God, we will not fear man. When we have been with Jesus, we won't surrender that intimacy to dance to another man's song. However, if we spend all our energy chasing after man's approval, there is no chance we can have God's. The most miserable Christian life is that of a man-pleaser. We try to live in the flesh, going off course and becoming unhappy, navigating our direction by accommodating our peers, critics, and supporters. We know what to do, but instead we spend our lives asking others what they think we *ought* to do. We ride a merry-go-round of repentance, regret, and recommitment. Pleasing man is spiritual fornication; Christ is trying to embrace His bride.

When we are living in Jesus, we are not directed by other people's opinions (positive or negative) but are filled with righteousness, peace, and joy, moved by the Holy Spirit. We can be like John Knox—the Queen of Scots trembled at his prayers.

Christ is not going to take a defeated church out of this world, nor will He come back to unanswered prayers or unfulfilled prophecies. Be assured that He is willing to kindle the fire of His life and mission in you. *You are part of Christ's end-time strategy!*

Satan's goal is to control and manipulate us, which he can only accomplish if we try to live this Christian life "sincerely" in our own strength. No matter how many Scriptures we quote or how devout our intentions are, Satan always has the upper hand when we walk in the flesh. We are called to be more than conquerors, but we have become, instead, Sunday warriors and Monday whiners.

Satan has no power over us when we allow the person of Christ to live through us. We're seated in heavenly places in Christ Jesus, and *it's not our flesh that is seated, it's our spirit*. When we're with Jesus, Satan will wear himself out trying to frustrate us and to unsuccessfully steal our peace and joy.

Jesus has called you into His kingdom and His glory (see 1 Thessalonians 2:12). We have been called into Christ's kingdom *on earth*. The battle Christ waged with Satan wasn't over God's kingdom in heaven; that was already firmly established—not subject to or in conflict with Satan. Rather, Christ defeated the devil to establish the kingdom of God *here and now*.

Satan fought to keep Jesus from this accomplishment. The devil is a master negotiator. When he offered the kingdoms of the world to Jesus (Matthew 4:8–9), he offered little: he knew Jesus could win even more. *Satan knew Jesus had the ability to establish His kingdom on earth, or he wouldn't have tempted him so greatly*.

Christ taught us to pray that God's kingdom would come and

that His will would be done on earth, as it is in heaven. When certain Greeks visiting Jerusalem desired to meet the Lord, they said to Philip, *"Sir, we would see Jesus"* (John 12:21). Jesus is alive on the earth today through you! Can others see Him in you? Have you seen Him by faith? Have you wrestled with God in prayer? The patriarch Jacob, whose name was changed to Israel, wrestled with a mysterious stranger until dawn and said, *"I have seen God face to face, and my life is preserved"* (Genesis 32:30). Prayer is the key.

We Cannot Live Without the Power of Prayer!

Go to the Killing Fields, Jesus directed me one day during prayer. No one had ever preached a nationwide crusade in the history of Cambodia, where more than two million people had been slaughtered in a horrific massacre almost rivaling the Holocaust. I took a humble pastor to Olympic Stadium in Cambodia and asked him, "Do you see it full?"

"No," he said. "There are only eighteen hundred Christians in the whole nation. This stadium may hold forty to sixty thousand. I see it empty."

"Close your eyes again and pray." We prayed for more than thirty minutes. Then he saw a thousand people in the stadium. We prayed again, and as he wept he said he saw five thousand people. He continued crying and praying until he could see the stadium packed full. Then I said, "Now it's time to have this crusade. Now that you've seen what Jesus sees, the person of the Holy Spirit will empower you so you can do what Jesus does."

God encouraged me to be bold with that totalitarian government. Through a divine miracle, the murderous Khmer Rouge approved the crusade, and tens of thousands of Buddhists and Khmer Rouge gathered together as we proclaimed the message of Jesus Christ—crucified, resurrected, and coming again. *It was the largest harvest of souls in the history of that nation.*

Jesus said we cannot live by bread alone (meaning the self life);

rather we live by every Word that proceeds out of the mouth of God. We have this power, yet we try to solve our problems ourselves! When we've been with Jesus, we are perfumed with prayer. We become God-wrestlers. The Word of God that proceeds out of our mouths causes hell to tremble.

In the midst of the greatest revival in the history of the world, in the manifest fullness of God's glory and power, something happened one day that even further revolutionized the apostles. They cried, *"We have to stop! We have to give ourselves to prayer!"* (see Acts 6:4). Prayer is fellowshipping with Jesus.

Why? Didn't the apostles know that everyone wanted to hear them preach and give their testimonies? This was the "big enchilada," the opportunity they'd waited for all these years. *Why slow down a revival to pray?* The disciples knew the blast of God's glory coming through them was supernatural, dynamic, shaking hell, and defeating principalities and powers. They would not jeopardize God's move by falling prey to the appetites of their flesh. They had to keep their spirits sharp by doing as they saw their Master do: Pray without ceasing.

Peter prophesied about the times of refreshing that would come; he knew with spiritual foresight that the day would arrive when others would figure out every key the apostles had learned to unlock revival. *They died to self.* They waited, tarrying in prayer, for God's Spirit to come upon them. When He did, they gave themselves to prayer. It is possible to pray without surrendering to Christ, but it is impossible to surrender to Christ without praying.

> *It is possible to pray without surrendering to Christ, but it is impossible to surrender to Christ without praying.*

Attempts to manipulate God rather than being with Jesus pass as "prayer" today. Often those who learn to "confess with their mouth" Christ's lordship never fully surrender to His authority in their hearts (see Romans 10:9). As a result, we enter into prayer without travailing and fasting.

> A woman when she is in travail hath sorrow, because her hour is come: but as soon as she is delivered of the child, she remembereth no more the anguish, for joy that a man is born into the world. (John 16:21)

We birth the present-day ministry of Jesus Christ with travailing prayer.

The fulfillment of our destiny comes through experiencing God's power, but we cannot have His power without His presence. We enter into God's presence through prayer! We do pray, so why don't we see His power? The great revivalist Leonard Ravenhill once said, "God does not answer prayer. God answers *desperate* prayer."

Only through prayer can we enter the intimate relationship with God for which He created us. Only through prayer can we truly wrestle with God.

Paul found the secret to spending time with God: "Pray without ceasing" (see 1 Thessalonians 5:17) and we will "be filled with all the fullness of God" (see Ephesians 3:14–19). Paul knew the power of the Holy Spirit and the deep love of Christ, which enabled him to fulfill God's purposes for him on earth. Every believer has this opportunity as well.

We say, "Lord, teach us to pray." How we need to learn to pray! To travail in desperate prayer! Again: If we do what we have done, we will have what we have had. If we want something we have never had, we have to do something we have never done.

A life without prayer is a life without purpose and power. One day fully surrendered to the purpose of God will reap more fruit than a lifetime lived with halfhearted intentions.

The Curse of Prayerlessness

Most American Christians are not praying "Jesus prayers" because they haven't *been* with Jesus. If fifty-seven million Christians *were* praying, the nation and the world would be changed. Prayer produces tremendous revivals. In Topeka, Kansas, students at a Bible school started to pray, and a revival broke out on the campus. Their prayer birthed the Azusa Street Awakening, which has brought millions into the baptism of the Holy Spirit and shaken the globe.

The average prayer time in the typical church service is relegated to the pastor or his associate, lasting two or three minutes. That's the extent of the prayer experienced by many in the congregation for the entire week! When a prayer meeting is called, it generally requires only the smallest room. The gymnasium is packed for basketball, the choir loft is filled for rehearsal, the classrooms are taken for myriad activities . . . and the prayer closet is practically empty.

I am convinced Christians do not pray because they do not believe. We do not believe that we're living in the end times. We do not believe that we are carrying destiny and the hope of glory. We do not believe that the Spirit of Christ within us will quicken our mortal bodies (Romans 8:11) or that we'll do greater things than Christ did because He ascended to the Father (John 14:12).

There is a marvelous realm of glory into which we are going to enter. Jesus said,

> I tell you that if two of you on earth agree about *any-thing* you ask for, it will be done for you by my Father in heaven. For where two or three come together *in my name,* there am I with them. (Matthew 18:19–20, emphasis added)

When we enter this realm, we are transported from praying and hoping God will do something to the realm of sitting together in heavenly places in Christ Jesus, watching Him do everything. No wonder the unsaved have run *from* the church rather than *to* the church. This will change. *They want help; they don't want hype.*

If we understood the dynamics and power of heaven, we

would pray. However, we understand neither the mission of the Holy Spirit nor the ultimate goal of Christ's intercession to the Father. We're tired of hearing *about* what God is going to do. We want to *see* it happen.

Some are praying. Thank God for a prayer movement that is bringing forth pockets of intercessors gathering for prayer around the world. But most believers are still not praying.

Of those who do pray, many try to use their faith and their energies to move God to answer their obscure prayers based on what they're going through or what they feel. The Bible says we don't even know how to pray. *The Spirit makes utterance for us so our prayers are based upon Jesus Christ—His mission, His kingdom, and His purposes.*

In the old Pentecostal days, if you had a problem, they'd tell you to "tarry" at the altar until you "prayed through." I went all night several times in those days and felt like I'd prayed only five minutes! "Praying through" means you *stay* in prayer until you are shut in with God in a secret place, getting sin and self out; closed in with God through the Spirit.

Samson, Israel's famous judge, relinquished to the enemy the secret of his fantastic strength and had his eyes gouged out. While enamored with his lover Delilah, he lost sight of the danger and was caught. As a slave grinding at the mill, he felt paralyzed from doing anything—even though he was actually empowered. We give up our secret place of prayer to an enemy who distracts, destroys, and robs us of the power to live victoriously. We are blind to our own weakened condition and the power available to us because we have been with everyone but Jesus.

When the disciples asked the Lord, "Why could we not cast [the demon] out?" His response was, "Because of your unbelief" (Matthew 17:19–20). *Prayerlessness is the bacteria growing the virus of unbelief.*

The entrance into God's presence is prayer. Jeremiah 29:13 reminds us, "Ye shall seek me, and find me, when ye shall search for me with all your heart."

We seem to make time for everything that interests us, even through sacrifice. But being shut in with God, and there beholding His face, is a rarity. Prayerlessness is a reproach to a loving God; prayer is our path to fellowship with Him. Without it, we are without direction and blindly guided by sensual appetites. *Praying in the Spirit while we are walking after the flesh is impossible.* The idea that a good service on Sunday—a "move of God"— fulfills our duty for the week is the very reason why demons do not tremble at our prayers!

Desperate prayer seeks the Father's face and is synonymous with being in the presence of Jesus. Desperate prayers are the prayers of God-wrestlers.

Let's Do It Again!

When the apostle Paul wrote of two becoming one, he wasn't speaking only of marriage but also of Christ and the bride (see Ephesians 5:31–32). Prayer is like marriage not because it's *similar,* but because God says it *is* marriage: Believers—the bride—are married to Christ, the Groom. Christ's power will be released through us as we consummate our union and draw close to Him.

We must endeavor not to assume we can be joined to Christ while denying Him intimacy. We must not tell Him we'll be married to Him while refusing to be alone with Him. *Intimacy is the mark of an authentic marriage.*

While holding a crusade in the Congo, I heard a testimony about J. W. Tucker, a missionary in the 1940s who was stoned for three hours until he died; his body was thrown into a river to be eaten by crocodiles. The tribe told the story through oral tradition (like a song or a proverb): "Listen to the testimony of J. W. Tucker, whose blood was shed in the river." Years later another missionary came and said to the people, "Will you listen to the testimony of J. W. Tucker, whose blood was shed in the river?" He shared it, and a great revival broke out in that village, with many souls converted.

The same thing will happen when Satan has to listen to the living witness of Jesus Christ, whose blood was shed on the cross—*we* become the torchbearers of that testimony. Such were the lives of biblical men like Moses, David, and Paul; the intimacy they achieved with God and the power demonstrated through their lives were consequences of their faithfulness. However, God's power is not reserved for "superstars of the faith"; it is, and always has been, available to every believer on earth. God is looking for those who will wrestle with Him.

You can accomplish more in one hour with Jesus on the throne of your life than in a lifetime without Him.

Remember: You can accomplish more in one hour with Jesus on the throne of your life than in a lifetime without Him.

Falling on our faces in prayer, armed with the understanding and revelation of God's Word, we can each achieve the power of the Cross, which has often appeared to be held in reserve for a few "choice vessels." All we have to do is get low with Christ.

"Praying through" is the channel that leads to being with Jesus. Let's pray through again! The Pensacola revival in Florida didn't start when evangelist Steve Hill came for a meeting. The release of power started years earlier when Pastor John Kilpatrick began to pray and cry out, "God, where are you?"

In the history of the world, humanity has never seen a revival that was not ushered in through prayer. The last great work of God on the earth will be no exception.

The Battle for the Anointing

Every time I have heard the voice of Jesus, it has been through prayer. One day Jesus softly spoke to my spirit: *You'll receive a phone call to go to the White House to pray for just one man. Give him this Scripture: "When you pass through the waters, I will be* with you; and through the rivers, they shall not overflow you. When you walk through the fire, you shall not be burned, nor shall the flame scorch you" (see Isaiah 43:2 NKJV).

A few days later an individual in the White House called and I went. I laid hands on a man I'd never seen before, and I gave him the Scripture God had given me. What a shock it was, within days, to see the man I had prayed for, Oliver North, on the front page of the newspaper, being called to congressional hearings. Several years later he told me he stood on that blessed Scripture throughout the whole ordeal.

It is *all* about Jesus and His present-day ministry, His taking us along as He goes about completing His mission on earth.

The anointing of Jesus Christ is not some type of Good Housekeeping seal of approval. We tend to believe that people, ministries, and maybe even denominations are anointed. But the Holy Spirit is not going about anointing a person, a ministry, or a denomination. *Jesus Christ is* the *Anointed One!*

The person of the Holy Spirit doesn't anoint organizations, no matter how much they attempt to live up to Christian principles; no blood flows down from the Cross for an institution. Jesus didn't die for an establishment—He died for people, individuals. *This doesn't mean that organizations are ungodly, it simply means we need to take extreme care not to exalt them.* The Holy Spirit doesn't affirm men or ministries; He has one goal, and that is to glorify the Father.

The Father wants the anointed ministry of Jesus Christ to function within us. He cannot move if we try to manipulate, control, or exploit His Holy Spirit. Jesus could indwell Mary, His earthly mother, because she didn't try to exploit Him. We are no threat to Satan if we don't allow the Lord's ministry to come forth. Until we fully yield our hearts to the lordship of Christ, following the leading of His Spirit, all our activities and good works are mere "saber rattling."

Corrie ten Boom, the concentration camp survivor who hid Jews in her home, once told me that the "secret place" in Psalm 91 means living before an audience of One. How many people live before an audience of One? Most believers want to be affirmed by other people, not by Christ.

People horribly misrepresent the Holy Spirit, saying things like "I prayed about it, and I have the witness [permission] of the Holy Spirit to get a divorce." If they want to destroy a person with their tongue, they say, "The Holy Spirit showed me that person isn't right with God." Such a misuse of the Spirit's name and position is damnable and despicable. Christ's ministry will not function in the lives of people who crucify Him again with their words. His precious blood is spewing all over the floor in the midst of these churches—not for lost souls, but because He has been executed afresh.

We have to win this battle over self-on-the-throne to receive the anointing of Christ flowing through us. Compromising Christians will be devoured and devastated in the final battle for souls. The contented and casual person will never be part of it, because the battle is waged on our knees. But for those in whom Christ fully manifests himself, we will never again be satisfied by living our lives without passion for God's glory.

Once again: *True intercession is not about "me," it's about "Him."* Intercession is focused on His needs, what's on His heart, what moves Him, what grieves Him, what His burdens are, what His passion is . . . *not "me" and "mine"*!

What-about-me Christianity breeds the bacteria of compromise. It turns preachers into prostitutes—every week they have to come up with a new trick to keep their congregations satisfied. God forbid a minister should stand up before his congregation and act like a human being, honestly admitting that he has been discouraged, or had an argument with his wife, or is dealing with anger. If he does, many so-called pillars of the church will likely nail him to the cross faster than Jesus was. Flesh wants to be noticed, wants to get credit, wants its "fair share," wants to be "treated right." If we try to save the lower life, we'll lose the higher one.

An open heart precedes an open heaven. The destiny of many lies in the hands of few. More than six billion people are depending on those who will die to self and allow the life of Christ to pour through them. Jesus said, "I, if I be lifted up from the earth, will draw all men unto me" (John 12:32). To lift Christ up, we must disconnect from this world's system.

God moves through prayer meetings. God's spotlight is looking for those who train their senses to turn away from the world and become hungry for Him, listening for sounds from heaven and smelling the fragrance of prayer as all eyes are focused on the Holy One. *This is the essence of wrestling with God.* The worshipers in King David's day turned their backs on the congregation, which symbolized flesh, and set their faces toward the ark of glory. The disciples saw the miracles and mighty works of Jesus, but they realized there is only one key to His power: prayer. Prayer bends the ear of God.

Power and Glory Only Through Prayer

Through prayer, Jesus once gently assured me that He would bring together Jewish and Christian leaders of our nation and that I was to announce the meeting. I did so at the next function I attended. Everyone there asked, "Where is it, and when?" I had to say I didn't know. I went home thinking that I had to find a place to hold the meeting, formulate a budget, and hire staff.

Don't say a word, I felt Jesus say as I prayed. *I am greater than you think. I am closer than you think. I am more committed than you think. I am more ambitious than you think.*

"God is greater than we think" became my topic several months later when I preached at the Orange Bowl. Bobbie James, the wife of Alabama's governor, came to me afterward and said she needed to fly me to her state because God told her He wanted to do something. Once there, as we prayed and she prophesied, the Lord told me I could share with her *His* vision. Alabama hosted the event the Lord had spoken to me about; they catered the food, brought in the Philharmonic Orchestra, and made it a truly wonderful meeting.

> *The present-day ministry of Jesus cannot operate under the controls of our flesh.*

I had been tempted to "help" God, doing it through my flesh so I could get the glory. The present-day ministry of Jesus cannot operate under the controls of our flesh.

We must see ourselves in the light of Christ and realize we can do nothing in our flesh. The Old Testament priest would stay up all night before he went into the Holy of Holies the next day, afraid to have even an unclean thought. Today we have Christian men by the thousands, the priests of their homes, who stay up all night to watch pornography on television or surf the Internet.

We must die to unbelief, lust, lying, cheating, impure thoughts, filthy speech, dirty habits, indifference, cursing, prayerlessness, envy, backbiting, selfishness, and bitterness . . . *anything* that is unholy and grieves the Holy Spirit. *Then* we can take a bold step into the Holy of Holies, trusting that Jesus will meet with us there:

> When thou prayest, enter into thy closet, and when thou hast shut thy door, pray to thy Father which is in secret; and thy Father which seeth in secret shall reward thee openly. (Matthew 6:6)

It's time to shut the door! The Holy Spirit is passionately attempting to capture your heart and mine. Christ wants to talk with us more than we want to talk with Him. The person of Jesus Christ is in *your* prayer closet, so enter into Him, abide in Him, and let Him abide in you. *Then* His magnificent voice will speak to you and through you.

When we abide in Christ, there will always be heavenly favor. We will know if the church is abiding in Christ by the size of the waves she makes around her. The victorious church is a battleship, not a luxury liner.

Beloved, it's time for us to realize *we are running either from God or to God.* When we've been with Jesus, we are marked for eternity, and when we are marked for eternity, we see clearly.

The person of the Holy Spirit is abiding in us, but He is too often imprisoned rather than impassioned within believers. The present-day ministry of Jesus is within reach of your hand, heart, and mind. We're not living in Old Testament times. It's not about anointed men. It's about *Immanuel,* Jesus, living and dwelling in us—until we are filled with the measure of the stature of the fullness of Christ.

The Father wants to show us Jesus and draw us to Jesus so we can be with Jesus. Revival cannot come to our lives, our homes, our churches, or our nation until we've been with Jesus.

CHAPTER FOUR

Don't Fake It!

For ye are dead, and your life is hid with Christ in God.
COLOSSIANS 3:3

As already mentioned, if we want something we've never had, we'll have to do something we've never done. Sadly, in the last decade it seems more Christians have left God than have come to Him. More books have been written about marriage than in all of church history, yet we're seeing the highest-ever rate of divorce. This is because we're propagating the falsehood that *we* can live the Christian life. The Christian life is not simply too hard to live in our flesh—*it is impossible.*

It's time to expose this lie! Christians are backsliding because they have been deceived. We try to overcome sin in our flesh, but the more we attempt to fight the hordes of hell with our strength, the more worried and discouraged we become. When we make up our *minds* not to allow flesh to control our lives, when the

Spirit power of Christ flows through us, *then* we will be delivered from struggles, worries, and fears, and we will go beyond anything we have ever imagined; we will enter into the greatest move of the Holy Spirit the world has ever seen. Flesh, no matter how sincere, can never break the chains of sin's power.

When we seek to live the Christian life on our own, we are as dry as desert sand. It's not about *our* stuff—vocation, education, gifts, power, personality, or intelligence. It's always about *His* stuff—kingdom, power, joy, grace, and peace. Any believer who thinks that in his strength he can overcome our unprecedented societal pollution, mass media seduction, and plague of demonic temptation is deceived.

We can cry a river of tears, pray with all our heart, and be sincerely in love with Jesus and at the same time be absolutely bound. We can ultimately surrender to a compromised Christianity; believing we can never be free from the power of sin, we resign ourselves to struggle in futility for the rest of our lives, sinning/repenting, sinning/repenting, sinning/repenting, and never becoming more than conquerors in Christ Jesus.

Like the believers in Laodicea, we begin to think lukewarmness is normal. When we subsequently experience the supernatural, we think it is abnormal; in fact, the miraculous is normal and lukewarmness is abnormal! Our flesh can never be better than tepid. Jesus said to the Laodicean Christians:

> "You are neither cold nor hot. I wish you were either one or the other! . . . Because you are lukewarm . . . I am about to spit you out of my mouth" (Revelation 3:15 NIV).

A multitude of believers have given up chasing the abundant Christian life. They speak faith, but in their hearts they don't believe it. Others are consumed with chasing after increased anointing, not realizing that the Anointed One abides within us. Once the obstacle is removed, glory *will* be manifest in our lives.

After we surrender to Him, the Savior rises up through the power of the Holy Spirit, and sin is stripped of its power by the

Spirit's glorious breath; only then can we truly know the meaning of victory in Jesus. Attempting to live the Christian life in our own flesh puts us at peace with our sin.

We must experience, as an act of our will, dying to our pride, boasting, ambitions, plans, and reputation. Only a Christian dead to the flesh and alive to Jesus can know the joy of being free from the power and dominion of sin.

> *Attempting to live the Christian life in our own flesh puts us at peace with our sin.*

It is only when we cry out to God in desperate surrender that the Holy Spirit can fully and completely fill us to overflowing, manifesting Jesus Christ in all His glorious resurrection power. The delegated ministry of Christ cannot be authorized or released from heaven, nor can we be empowered as long as we attempt to *reform the flesh* instead of being with Jesus.

We have not been called to win the world for Christ. We have been called to die so that He can live through us to win the world to himself through us. I have preached all over the world, and I have seen that no one can preach eloquently enough, neither can musicians sing well enough, to lead the world to the Lord. An open heaven caused a church of 120 to see three thousand people converted in one day, sparking the most amazing revival in history (recorded in the book of Acts)! To God be the glory; it will happen again in our day in an even more overwhelming dimension.

The Elusive Brass Ring

We've all wondered, "Why do miracles happen for some and not for others?" For years I felt like I was circling a merry-go-round with my hand out, occasionally grasping the brass ring. I thought supernatural events were a sign of God's affirmation and approval of me, as if He were saying, *"You're doing so well, here's a miracle."* When I became discouraged, depressed, and driven to my knees in desperate prayer, the power surge came, but I thought God was just saying, *"Cheer up, kid."* Oh, the ego of it all! The person of the Holy Spirit cannot and will not be used as an endorsement or affirmation of anyone or anything other than Christ's own ministry!

Jesus said, "Abide in me, and I in you. As the branch cannot bear fruit of itself, except it abide in the vine; no more can ye, except ye abide in me. . . . For without me ye can do nothing" (John 15:4–5). Jesus meant that none of what we do amounts to anything apart from Him. We can accomplish nothing redemptive with our flesh (no matter how religious we are or seem to be), nothing that causes demons to tremble, and nothing that builds eternity.

> *The person of the Holy Spirit cannot and will not be used as an endorsement or affirmation of anyone or anything other than Christ's own ministry!*

The apostle Paul had "no confidence in the flesh" (Philippians 3:3).

It took me a long time to correlate my dying to Christ's living. God wasn't saying, *"Cheer up."* He was saying, *"See what I can do through you when you acknowledge you can't do anything?"* God did not start the Pensacola revival to cheer up a depressed pastor. He visited when John Kilpatrick came to the end of his spiritual rope and, from a pure heart, called out to the Lord for help. Miracles are not an endorsement of *our efforts* but the very signature of the Holy Spirit validating the present-day ministry of Jesus Christ.

It is never about us; it is always about Him! Yet round and round we go, operating on false assumptions and asking Christ to "assist" us. Since we retain control, that's the only role we have available to "give" Him. The arrogance of this astonishing thinking is humiliating. Christianity is not about pulling ourselves up by our bootstraps or trying harder. *Christianity is acknowledging that apart from Him, we can do nothing.* Paul didn't put less confidence in the flesh. He put *no* confidence in the flesh. *Zero.*

We will never do the greater things if all we do is attempt to use Jesus Christ as some kind of outside resource.

The Fruit, Not the Root

Sin is not our only problem. *Flesh is carried away by lust that brings about sin* (see James 1:15). Sin is the fruit; flesh is the root. When we repent of sin, we're dealing with the fruit, which is very important. But the root—self on the throne—is even more critical.

The Holy Spirit gives us the power to see our flesh from an eternal perspective. Flesh-fed Christians sometimes observe: "There is now no condemnation for those who are in Christ Jesus" (Romans 8:1 NIV). However, that passage also says, *"who live [and] walk not after the dictates of the flesh, but after the dictates of the Spirit"* (AMP).

To understand the work of Christ on the cross, we must understand the total depravity of our flesh. Flesh is the external part of us: the carnal, the earthy, the worldly, the passions and desires of the human nature. Flesh is the nonspiritual, unbridled, and unharnessed in us. *Flesh is the fallen self.* More than anything, flesh is our ego—the part of us that desires control and recognition. It has its own agenda and insists upon its own way.

The fact that Jesus came to earth in the flesh is not a coincidence. He became flesh for us, and He said,

> "I am the living bread which came down from heaven: if any man eat of this bread, he shall live for ever: and the bread that I will give is my flesh, which I will give for the life of the world" (John 6:51).

Jesus Christ, the sinless Son of God, came *in* the flesh in order to conquer flesh so that He could live *through* us, giving us victory *over* the flesh. This is the significance of Jacob's wrestling match.

Many scholars believe the "man" with whom Jacob wrestled in Peniel was the Lord and that His appearance was a theophany (an Old Testament manifestation of deity). Genesis 32:25 says, "He *touched* the hollow of his thigh; and the hollow of Jacob's thigh was out of joint, as he wrestled with him" (emphasis added). Intimacy with Christ means our flesh is confronted and the Spirit is empowered. *God-wrestling brings about a changed life.* Jacob became Israel, but he walked with a limp for the rest of his life.

Adam was created by God to have dominion over the earth and fellowship with his Creator. But Adam granted lordship to his flesh. As a result, sin corrupted him, and the pure communication between God and man was spoiled. *The only way fellowship could be restored was for God to come in the flesh to conquer sin and restore humankind to its rightful place* (see Romans 8:3). This is why Jesus is called the "Second Adam" (or "son of Adam," *Ben Adam*).

Jesus saw the flesh as the supreme enemy of God (see Hebrews 5:7; 10:20). By shedding his blood on Calvary, Christ not only saved our souls and provided healing for our bodies, He also granted us power over the flesh.

A biblical revelation has been hidden from the eyes of many of us in the church.

> Therefore, I urge you, brothers, in view of God's mercy, to offer your bodies as living sacrifices, holy and pleasing to God—this is your spiritual act of worship. (Romans 12:1 NIV)

The priests offered animals on the altar; Christ offered himself as the sinless God-man. We are to offer our bodies—the self life—as a living sacrifice, because the Lord knew:

Flesh cannot inherit the kingdom of God (see 1 Corinthians 6:9–10).

Flesh lusts against the spirit (see Galatians 5:17).

The natural person, ruled by the flesh, cannot submit to God's will or please Him (see Romans 8:7–8).

Our flesh is weak (see Matthew 26:41).
Our flesh desires to enslave us (see Ephesians 2:3).
There is no righteous flesh (see Romans 6:20).
No matter how religious, flesh is flesh (see Galatians 2:16).

Even demons had to acknowledge that Jesus had come in the flesh (see Mark 3:11). "Many deceivers, who do not acknowledge Jesus Christ as coming in the flesh, have gone out into the world" (2 John 1:7 NIV). Paul understood the amazing power of Christ to deliver us from the controlling power of our flesh through dying, so that we can "sit together in heavenly places in Christ Jesus" (Ephesians 2:6) to fulfill His present-day ministry. This revelation made Paul a mighty warrior and a God-wrestler! He lived in a state of constant awareness, which put him in a place of constant readiness.

A mighty deliverer, a mighty conqueror, lives and dwells inside us—the Supreme King who has already conquered everything and has everything we need to overcome our flesh.

Christ, the Word, became flesh to die *to* the flesh so that we might be delivered *from* the flesh. Recognizing He was flesh, Jesus went to a repentance service conducted by John the Baptist. John was mortified that the Son of the living God wanted to be baptized by him, but Jesus said, "Let it be so now; it is proper for us to do this to fulfill all righteousness" (Matthew 3:15 NIV). Jesus submitted to a baptism of repentance even though He had committed no sin!

The Bible says, "The Word was made flesh, and dwelt among us" (John 1:14). *That Word is Jesus.* Even though He is fully God and absolutely sinless, He died through the baptism of repentance so that He, as our exemplar, could rise up in the fullness of the Spirit. When Jesus died to the flesh through baptism, the heavens opened up and the Father said, "This is my beloved Son, in whom I am well pleased" (Matthew 3:17). Supernaturally, the Holy Spirit descended as a dove upon the sinless Jesus Christ, who had been submerged into the waters of repentance to die to the flesh for all humankind to see.

The Leprosy of Fleshly Living

Fleshly living on the throne of our lives always refuses to allow the person of the Holy Spirit to have the final word. The consequence is that Christians are living in a perpetual cycle of defeat and hypocrisy. Why did Christ choose to abide in a fleshly body and die to that flesh while He lived? He has a plan to sanctify our flesh, through the power of the Holy Spirit, so that He can manifest and demonstrate His present-day ministry to shake the world like it has never been shaken.

King Uzziah of Judah "sought God in the days of Zechariah. . . . And *as long as he sought the* LORD*, God made him to prosper*" (2 Chronicles 26:5, emphasis added). However, after reigning many years, Uzziah made himself a censer that he filled with his own fire rather than with the consecrated fire at the altar. As he marched to the temple to function as a self-appointed priest, the priests blocked his way, but he raged at them. In the midst of his fleshly outburst, leprosy broke out on his forehead and he hurried from the temple.

This mighty king, beloved of the prophets Isaiah and Zechariah, became filled with flesh, intoxicated by his own reputation and religiously proud of striving to do what he thought was right. He said, in essence, "I'm as holy as any priest. I've done so many good works that there's no reason I can't come into the presence of God." His life ended tragically: "Uzziah the king was a leper unto the day of his death" (2 Chronicles 26:21).

When the Spirit of Christ dealt with me at the peak of "my" ministry, He said, *You are competing for my blood.* Essentially, I was attempting to be righteous and spiritual in my own strength rather than realizing that my righteousness and spirituality amounted to nothing. When we attempt to live a "good life" through our own efforts and resist sin by using our own flesh, we insult the Great High Priest (Christ) just as King Uzziah did. We are basically saying, "Step aside, Lamb of God, as I exalt this flesh on the altar."

No matter how hard we try in our own power, no matter

how much encouragement we receive from friends to be strong and victorious, if we attempt to live the Christian life by our own resources, the leprosy of sin will continually fester.

Jesus' Flesh Defeated Flesh

Christ came in the flesh, defeated the flesh, and conquered the flesh in His own glory. His work on the cross delivers us from our flesh, and His blood delivers us from our sins, providing healing for our sick bodies.

Through His baptism, death, and resurrection, Jesus precisely mapped out what we must do to be glorified with Him. Jesus humbled himself and died to the flesh through the baptism of repentance when the heavens opened. The heavens will likewise open for us when we follow the Savior's pattern. Christianity has never been about living *for* Christ but about dying *with* Christ. God cannot resurrect living flesh, only dead flesh.

When our flesh decreases, Christ will increase.

The Spirit of God told me to go to El Salvador and hold a crusade in just thirty-one days. People pleaded with me not to rush, but I went. As I ate breakfast with the minister of the interior, Jesus softly told me to meet with the president. I instantly jumped up from the hotel restaurant and ran toward the front door, not knowing where I was going but inadvertently bumping directly into the entourage of the president himself! When we met later, along with his secretary of state, a general in the meeting wrote "2 Chronicles 7:14" on his hand as I quoted it. Embroiled in a civil war, the president agreed to call for national prayer and fasting. The war ended shortly thereafter.

Godly Christians in that nation had been praying, and God graciously answered their prayers. A great revival broke out. I was invited to speak on a television program and given the entire morning to preach the gospel after one of the hosts was healed by God's power. News spread, and the vice president's wife called me to the palace. On the way, Jesus gently instructed me to stop the military escort and pray for a crippled old man on the side of the heavily congested road. I replied, "Yes, Lord, after I pray for the vice president's wife."

When I arrived at the palace, Jesus said, *If you're going in, you're going alone. Go back now and pray for the man.*

I excused myself, and we plowed back through traffic to where we had seen the precious handicapped man. As we drove, the power of God fell so mightily upon me that I knew that I knew that I knew Christ was walking in me, talking in me, and reaching through me. When I got out of the car, I said to the man, "*Señor,* such as I have, I give unto thee. In the name of Jesus of Nazareth, rise up and be healed."

He threw his canes over his head and started running up and down the street, screaming, "I'M HEALED!" Cars by the dozens had their windows rolled down, and the motorists were crying and shouting, *"I believe in Jesus!"* and *"I believe in God!"*

His agenda. Not our agenda. Christ died *to* the flesh, and then He died *in* the flesh, so we would follow Him and live *in the Spirit.*

Glorified Flesh Restored

When Jesus arose, He appeared to His disciples and said, "Touch me and see; a ghost does not have flesh and bones, as you see I have" (Luke 24:39 NIV). His disciples had to see that He was alive in the flesh because they thought He was solely a spirit! Jesus Christ restored flesh to the holiness in which Adam was originally created. Before His crucifixion, Christ offered the first communion; as He broke the bread, He said, "This is my body" (Luke 22:19). In other words, "Eat my flesh." The bread was symbolic of His body, offered (sacrificed) to save us from our flesh.

We cannot deodorize, clean, or perfume our flesh to make it acceptable to God. The disciples eventually gave up trying while living with Jesus, realizing that "no flesh should glory in God's presence" (1 Corinthians 1:29). They acknowledged their failure and realized their efforts were insufficient: "Lord, teach us to pray" (Luke 11:1).

We try to disguise or cleanse our flesh with good works, but to God, flesh stinks! The flesh says, "God, I'm doing this for you. Bless it." *God only blesses what He authors and what He will finish, as well* (see Hebrews 12:2). Why would Jesus want to do anything with us if He isn't allowed to manage His own mission?

Control, micromanaging, and guardedness in a believer's life all make this statement: "I refuse to trust Christ with my self because He might mess it up. I have to be careful not to empty my self and give Him complete access."

To refuse to surrender to Jesus Christ is to war against His lordship. We sing one thing on Sundays but refuse all week to speak to others about Christ . . . or to tithe . . . or to ask someone for forgiveness. The desire for control in any area of our lives hinders the present-day ministry of Jesus.

Does Christianity Even Work?

At the point of salvation, we give God authority over our lives, but then we often live oppositely and wonder why we can't live victoriously. We should ask ourselves the question, "Does Christianity work?"

In praying over this book, the Lord has raked me over the coals with embarrassing and humiliating conviction. I can't imagine how my sins must appear to a holy God. The truth is, my flesh doesn't want to die. Jesus has shown me that *dying to self requires tears, and only we can shed those tears.*

Jesus can't live triumphantly through a Christian who allows self to rule. He has already died for that believer; He cannot die again. *We* have to die. When the flesh dies, it cries.

A gospel with perversion cannot bring conversion. We can quote Scriptures until we become a walking Bible, but demons will not tremble and the world will not be changed. *The moment self is dethroned and we passionately, insatiably pursue a relationship with Jesus, the Word will become fire in our bones.*

We must humbly admit that most of us are attempting to live the Christian life in our own strength—the greatest obstacle to releasing the glory of God. Religion is futilely determined to clean up self until it's acceptable, sanitized, and sweet-smelling.

Without dying to our flesh, we are simply religious clones, trying to copy others. Religion without Jesus polishes, franchises, and mass-markets self, doing everything but dethroning the idol. If religion keeps self intact, then religion itself must be dethroned.

When self is dethroned, the fire of God will be felt in our lives. Satan will be vanquished and we will proclaim Christ as victor. No wonder the enemy of our soul fights to pamper, powder, and prosper our self life so that the sweet spirit of Jesus cannot break us.

> *We must humbly admit that most of us are attempting to live the Christian life in our own strength—the greatest obstacle to releasing the glory of God.*

Satan's greatest fear is the child of God who has been with Jesus; one who is completely yielded to the holy fire of the living God and fully manifesting His glory. The casual Christian cannot be lit up. Religion cannot deliver our families, our nation, our world, or us. There is no time left to play the part. There is only time to *be* the part.

Satan has found the key to keep at bay the most powerful force in the universe. Christ is fully authorized by the Father to manifest His glory to a lost and dying world. The devil can't stop Him because Jesus has already won that battle. But we can. Jesus will not empower our flesh to sit in control of our lives and make a mockery of His sacrifice.

The Big Lie

While I was having dinner several years ago with former U.N. Ambassador Jeanne Kirkpatrick, the conversation turned to Hitler and the Holocaust. I asked her, based on all her studies, how she thought Hitler was able to deceive the world. Jeanne responded, "Because Hitler told such a big lie."

The size of the lie made it work! A little lie could not have accomplished what a big lie could. Over six million Jews were exterminated after Hitler propagated a deception so massive that most people were fooled; they didn't believe anyone would dare lie so brazenly. The big lie was that he was going to kill all the Jews in Europe.

Satan, the father of lies, has propagated *the* big lie. He knew a power infusion was coming, which, through Christ, would wipe him out forever. He knew Jesus had sent to the church the powerful Holy Spirit that raised Him from the dead. He knew Jesus delegated to us all His power and authority. He also knew he couldn't neutralize believers by selling us on something as obvious as cultic free-sex practices. Satan's invented deception is "You can be a good Christian."

On the surface, those words don't sound false. To the contrary, they sound so correct, so righteous, so ideal, so godly—they must be true! Then Satan adds, "You can reform your flesh." It's a lie.

The church has not widely exposed this insidious deception. We've been seduced to think, *Now that I'm a Christian, my flesh is good.* This is a falsehood with one primary objective: Keep the flesh alive and in control. The result? We cause Christ to lose the battle of lordship in our lives!

The reason we have not overcome the world, and the reason God's glory has not shaken our cities, is that we've believed a lie. We think we can improve ourselves through good works and rescue self from the dominion of our flesh. Until we are willing to admit how wicked and sinful our flesh is and how empty and helpless we are to deliver ourselves, we can never be rescued.

The greatest threat to Satan's kingdom is dethroned flesh. Flesh cannot go after God because it doesn't have zeal or an urgency for Him. When we dethrone the flesh, we can have intimacy with our Creator. We then understand how much He enjoys our fellowship. We don't find our identity through ironclad rules. We accomplish more in one day of living a crucified life than in a lifetime of sincere religious intentions.

Satan is preparing his greatest onslaught; he endeavors to take hostage and keep prisoner the generation that will see the Lord's appearing, knowing the key battle for our souls lies in keeping us blinded by the flesh. "Let not the wise man glory in his wisdom," the Lord says, "neither let the mighty man glory in his might, [and] let not the rich man glory in his riches" (Jeremiah 9:23).

> *We accomplish more in one day of living a crucified life than in a lifetime of sincere religious intentions.*

Corrupt Flesh

The flesh is utterly corrupt. "God looked upon the earth, and, behold, it was corrupt; for all flesh had corrupted his way upon the earth" (Genesis 6:12). When God instituted the sacrifice for sins, the flesh of animals was burned symbolically so we could understand its worthlessness (see Leviticus 7:17).

God chastised the Israelites for desiring meat (see Numbers 11:13). Our world system craves flesh. Even our religious appetites are fleshly. We seek the praise of men, the opinions of men, and the favor of men. God cannot abide our insatiable appetite for flesh.

All God's powerful leaders understood flesh was powerless. King Hezekiah proclaimed, "With him [the king of Assyria] is an arm of flesh; but with us is the LORD our God to help us, and to fight our battles" (2 Chronicles 32:8). Jeremiah cried, "Thus saith the LORD; *cursed be the man that trusteth in man,* and maketh flesh his arm, and whose heart departeth from the LORD'" (Jeremiah 17:5, emphasis added).

Jesus said, "It is the spirit that quickeneth; *the flesh profiteth nothing:* the words that I speak unto you, they are spirit, and they are life" (John 6:63, emphasis added). He also clarified the new birth: "That which is born of the flesh is flesh; and that which is born of the Spirit is spirit" (John 3:6).

Can *our* flesh be saved? No! The day before we knew Christ, we had corruptible flesh; the day after we met Him, we still had corruptible flesh . . . but *then* we had Christ living within us.

The Bible says, "Flesh and blood cannot inherit the kingdom of God" (1 Corinthians 15:50). When Christ comes again, our flesh is not going with us into the presence of the Holy One. In God's eyes, no flesh is clean, and flesh cannot please God (see Romans 8:4–8). Paul understood this: "I know that in me (that is, in my flesh) dwelleth no good thing" (Romans 7:18).

We've tried to please God in our own flesh, creating a fake-it-till-we-make-it Christian mentality. We keep trying to fix our flesh. Since it can't be fixed, we leave ourselves no choice but to fake it. Spouses in a marriage who fake intimacy eventually give up. In the same way, Christians who fake the victorious Christian life eventually quit on the church. The result of living after the flesh is death. Death in our churches is rampant: through backsliding, scandal, divorce, congregational splits, and closures.

Being with Jesus is not about another program or entertainment designed to motivate us. *Being with Jesus is about dying to the flesh.* Every fire-filled saint who shook his world and his generation, whether in biblical or other historical records, shook it only because he had been with Jesus. Smith Wigglesworth was considered one of the most pathetic preachers of his day, yet he raised the dead. William Seymour was derided, mocked, and considered an ignorant moron, yet he was the instrument used by Jesus to birth the Pentecostal fires in which more than six hundred million people worldwide have been baptized in the Holy Spirit!

The apostle Paul told us to mortify the deeds of the body by putting on the Lord Jesus Christ and making no provision for the flesh (see Romans 8:13; 13:14). When we are confident of Christ's exceeding greatness in us, we don't need to feed on fleshly compliments or have our flesh pumped up. "There is therefore now no condemnation to them which are in Christ Jesus, who walk not after the flesh, but after the Spirit" (Romans 8:1). If we don't pursue the flesh, we cannot be condemned. That spells freedom!

Flesh Community Church

Paul said, "Walk in the Spirit, and ye shall not fulfill the lust of the flesh" (Galatians 5:16). Our minds, in contrast to being filled with wisdom, are saturated with filth from all forms of marketing and entertainment. We have been seduced into believing that right is wrong and wrong is right. Some in the church now promote a gospel that does not convict humankind of sin. Others are embarrassed at the concepts of intercession and holiness as if these were hopelessly out-of-date.

We are walking blindfolded on the edge of eternity because we have allowed our hearts to become desensitized to the gentle person of the Holy Spirit. That's how the Bible becomes merely the tool of our trade, and we are no longer ruled by compassion but instead by the whims of the flesh. All the while, angels weep and demons rejoice.

When we accept and accommodate the flesh, in essence we create "Flesh Community Church." Flesh Community Church grows to ten thousand members, and then others say, "Let's copy them; they're successful." Yet some of the leaders of the biggest ministry "successes" have fallen victim to the very flesh they tolerated.

As they left the temple one day, the disciples asked Jesus, "What will be the sign of your coming and of the end of the age?" Jesus replied, "Watch out that no one deceives you. For many will come in my name, saying, 'I am the Christ'" (Matthew 24:3–4 NIV). This is not *the* antichrist, for the antichrist is one man. Christ is speaking of the *spirit* of antichrist.

Jesus said many would come in His name, which means His

reputation, authority, and fame. The word *I* refers to "ego," and *Christ* means "the Anointed One." Jesus was saying, *"Take another look, so that no one can deceive you, for many will come in my reputation, authority, and fame, saying 'I am (my ego is) anointed.'"* Jesus said many would come in their flesh, their own ego, using His name and acting as though their lives were empowered by Him!

Christ wants to manifest His ministry through us, but our flesh is battling the birthing process. Satan's great challenge to God was all about ego: "*I* will ascend; *I* will exalt; *I* will sit; *I* will be." God responded, *"Thou shalt be brought down to hell, to the sides of the pit"* (see Isaiah 14:12–15).

Satan was determined to be in control. He looked at God's throne and said, "I will exalt *my* throne above the stars." If God allows our flesh to take control of our lives, and Christianity to be something we do on Sundays, Jesus being subjugated to second place, then Lucifer ("Son of the Morning"), whom God cut down, deserves, in my opinion, a second chance! Was his sin greater? He won't get a second chance, but we shouldn't forget it. *God has been merciful with us.*

To God be the glory for how magnificently the Christ life can be lived when we die to our flesh; then, and only then, can ordinary Christians become a manifestation, a blast, of God's glory.

If the apostles living with Jesus were utter failures until they died to their flesh, why do we presume we don't have to die to ours? As long as sincere, well-meaning Christian flesh rules and reigns, compromise will be as common as breath.

Cicero said, "A nation can survive its fools and even the ambitious, but it cannot survive treason from within." America and the world are speeding toward a Christless eternity; nothing can stop us but a heavenly visitation.

The prophet Jeremiah recorded the Lord as saying, "Can . . . the leopard [change] its spots? Neither can you do good who are accustomed to doing evil" (Jeremiah 13:23 NIV). There is no room for flesh in the Spirit-led life! Author Ed Cole says, "The flesh will always conspire with the world to turn you over to the hands of the devil."

God said to hate "even the garment [the outerwear] spotted by the flesh" (Jude 23). How can we think we can live our Christian life by religious accomplishments or by the accolades of our peers? Even our willpower is still flesh! Not even the most gifted and accomplished flesh can glory, because *all* flesh is silenced in the presence of a holy God.

Satan's greatest hope is that Christians live in the flesh, with all the good intentions that accompany a tear-filled conversion. God does *not* want us to attempt to bring our flesh under control and then offer it up to Him as pleasing in His sight.

The secret to the Christ life is not trying to conform our flesh to a set of religious standards. I tried that. It was a festival of hypocrisy in the theater of the absurd and a prescription for a defeated Christian life. That which is born of flesh is flesh. God is not trying to change our flesh! *God wants to take us beyond the flesh, to cause the flesh to lose its power and control, so we can be seated together in heavenly places with Christ Jesus.* We must stop pumping "flat fix" into the tired old tires of religious flesh—it's a worthless effort.

We have been educated by a world system to have self-confidence, self-respect, and self-esteem—all of which concentrates on self, if not exalts it. When we walk in the Spirit, surrendering our lives to Jesus, we walk in *His* confidence. God-confidence supersedes self-confidence.

When we're *self*-conscious, we often become depressed because we're centered on the ego. We become frustrated because we are focusing on what is happening to us. We become offended, angry, and irritated. Everything revolves around how it affects *me*. We cannot live the victorious Christian life if we haven't been with Jesus, and the reason we haven't been with Jesus is that our self hasn't been upstaged.

The world in modern times has essentially seen nothing but a prescription for failure called "the Christian life." And they don't want it! Yet ordinary people like Corrie ten Boom and Mother Teresa have already proved that if we'll empty our self to live the Christ life *unhindered,* the world will follow us to the Father in droves.

The Lord asks us, *"Do you trust me? Then let me live my life unhindered in you."* A yielded soul is fertile soil for a heavenly harvest.

Attempting to reform the flesh is shaking a fist at the Cross of Calvary and shouting, "We're not so bad!" Jesus would not have come to earth if we had the ability to become good enough to enter the presence of a holy God.

Contemporary Christians are not unlike the Israelites, who went through the motions of religious service to an empty ark while keeping "high places" for idolatrous worship during the week. When we allow flesh to glorify flesh, we engage in idolatry.

I found I had no wisdom, ability, or strength to accomplish any such thing. Instead, once the Holy Spirit knew that I had exhausted my own efforts, He released the ministry of Jesus Christ through me like I've seldom seen. This should be the norm!

Christianity Works!

Christianity *does* work. When we try to live our Christian lives in our own strength and power, however, we propagate a miserable failure.

Christianity was working when William Seymour—a poor, one-eyed, discriminated-against African-American who had been with Jesus—started one of the twentieth century's greatest movements. The Azusa Street Revival that sprang out of his singular devotion to God is one of the most strategic victories in Christian history. The gospel can be seen, not just heard, when it is embraced in the heart of the believer.

CHAPTER FIVE

For Hungry and Thirsty Christians Only

God anointed Jesus of Nazareth with the Holy Ghost and with power . . . for God was with Him.
ACTS 10:38

The driving passion of our hearts must be to know Jesus fully and to allow Him to live His life through us according to *His* purpose, not ours. We are hungry and thirsty, wanting to say with all honesty to a lost and dying world, "I've been with Jesus." It is only being with Jesus that *will* qualify us for the last great visitation, which will take us beyond anything we have ever experienced.

As Christians, we have seen glimpses of Christ's ministry unhindered, but except for a few revivals here and there, we haven't seen an outpouring of God's power as on the Day of

Pentecost since . . . well . . . Pentecost! The life of Christ within us is much larger than the random power surge, and the ultimate work of God will be much more wondrous than isolated incidents. *Ordinary Christians are about to experience the unbelievable, behold the unthinkable, and witness book-of-Acts miracles.*

Why Stand Gazing?

The apostle Paul turned the fleshly Roman Empire upside down. He didn't fight with the flesh's weapons of war—legalism, pride, arrogance, unbridled passions—but instead operated within the present-day ministry of Christ.

Our works will be judged either as precious jewels or as wood, hay, and stubble. If we have not surrendered to Jesus, we will not be a glorious church without spot or wrinkle; we will have a wedding dress that is dirty, wrinkled, and torn, worn by an unembarrassed bride who is still ignorantly anticipating the union with enthusiasm. If our works are worthless and have to be burned, we will find ourselves knee-deep in ashes for our contemporary exaltation of the flesh.

We're so busy struggling to live our own Christian life that we have little energy for outrage. "Lord, help!" we cry. "Help us, Jesus!" The Bible says,

> He is able (immediately) to run to the cry of (assist, relieve) those who are being tempted and tested and tried [and who therefore are being exposed to suffering]. (Hebrews 2:18 AMP)

If Christ *is* helping, why are so many Christians mired in such hellish conditions? If Christ is with us, why are so many backsliding and being taken off our church rolls? If Christ is in us, why are over three thousand churches closed every year?

"Why stand ye gazing up into heaven?" the angels asked those who had watched Christ's ascension (Acts 1:11). It's time that God delivers us from heaven-gazers! Gazers pollute God's purposes because they *look* into the sky but *live* by their own agendas. They short-circuit His power in thinking Jesus is "up there, somewhere" because their motivation is to empower flesh. If Christ were to empower gazers with self on the throne, He would make a mockery of the sacrifice He offered at Calvary.

The refusal to surrender complete control of our lives to Christ is a blatant declaration of war against His lordship.

> *The refusal to surrender complete control of our lives to Christ is a blatant declaration of war against His lordship.*

I missed it in the 1980s when I served on the executive committee of "Washington for Jesus" with Pat Robertson, Paul Crouch, and a half dozen other evangelical leaders. We thought we could bring about a spiritual awakening in America by instilling Christian values in government. I also served on the executive committe for the American Coalition for Traditional Values with Jerry Falwell and Tim LaHaye. We worked with 220,000 churches, believing we could help. But we missed it. Simply missed it.

The White House is not the key to revival—the church is! Jesus does not reside in the White House; Jesus resides in the body of believers, *His* body. When Paul spoke of marriage as a union between a man and his wife, he said, "This is a great mystery: but I speak concerning Christ and the church" (Ephesians 5:32). There is a spiritual union and an ignition point—a Spirit-to-spirit contact between Christ and His church—that births the manifestation of God's glory.

William Seymour reflected,

> We wonder why sinners are not being converted, and why the church is always making improvements, and failing to do the work that Christ has called her to do. It is because men have taken the place of Christ and His Holy Spirit.

Instead of shutting ourselves in with Jesus, we run to meetings. We listen to this person who is "anointed" or that person who hears from God, or this tape series our friends told us about or that video we saw advertised. We rejoice over everyone else's victories and may even experience some of our own. But Scripture says we are to become "more than conquerors" (Romans 8:37). We don't continually experience the more-than-conquerors lifestyle.

The present-day ministry of Jesus Christ is always in the *now*. We must take our seat beside the High Priest—Jesus, our elder brother—to rule and reign with Him in the now. It's time to stop talking about doing His stuff and start doing it.

God, I'm Hungry, and I Want to Know You

"God, I'm hungry. I want to know you. Will you use me?" Such were my prayers in Jerusalem on February 17, 1993, when He gave me a dramatic vision of a revival that will change the destiny of the world. It is not about a man, an activity, or an idea. Christians have been obsessed with finding new ways to save face or put on a new face, but the obsession of the believers who will usher in Christ's coming and reap the final harvest will be seeking *His* face.

The vision God gave me contained very specific prophecies: Among them, the resignation of Boris Yeltsin before the year 2000. I was amazed on December 31, 1999, when news broadcasts interrupted New Year's celebrations worldwide with a special bulletin: "Boris Yeltsin, in a surprise move, has stepped down and named his successor."

God showed me believers manifesting His glory more magnificently than the world has ever seen, with His power revealed until millions are called into the ministry and all the gifts of the Spirit are fully functioning. The power will be increased until believers are filled up with the fullness of God.

God showed me a river of revival springing up in America by an unknown evangelist and pastor. This revival is the "first fruit," a foreshadowing of a supernatural move greater than any revival, empowering Christ's body of believers, the church, to release His present-day ministry and ultimately usher in His return. *God showed me that this final movement will be marked by greater intimacy between Jesus and believers and by a river of repentance resulting in millions of souls coming into the kingdom. Hallelujah!*

God wants to send a mighty fire today to burn up fleshly arrogance, to make His saints combustible, saturated with the oil of the Holy Spirit, lit on fire for His glory and mobilized for battle. In the book of Acts, pastors and evangelists weren't the ministers. Everyone who named Jesus Christ as Lord was a minister of the Gospel, a holy flame. God wants to pour that kind of anointing out today, so there will be no *big I* and *little you.*

What must we do to be empowered to fulfill Christ's mission on earth?

God, Where Are You?

Pray for the peace of Jerusalem (Psalm 122:6).

After sixty-one days of fasting and prayer, God spoke the vision for the Jerusalem Prayer Team into my heart. This was to be God's dream and God's team. After I heard from heaven, I flew to Jerusalem to meet with Mayor Ehud Olmert to share the vision of the Jerusalem Prayer Team. He was greatly touched and flew to Dallas in June 2002 to inaugurate this prayer movement. Dr. Franklin Graham, Dr. Jerry Falwell, former Prime Minister Benjamin Netanyahu, Representative Dick Armey, and Governor Rick Perry were some of those who participated either by letter or video.

Christians from all over America and around the world have joined the Jerusalem Prayer Team. Many are household names, including Dr. Tim LaHaye, Dr. Pat Robertson, Mr. Bill McCartney, Dr. John Maxwell, Mr. Pat Boone, Ms. Kay Arthur, Mrs. Anne Graham Lotz, Dr. Jerry Falwell, Rev. Tommy Tenney, and over three hundred national leaders in America and thousands worldwide.

September 11, 2001, was a tragic day in American history. It was a physical manifestation of a battle that had been lost weeks, months, and possibly years before, because of a lack of prayer. Osama bin Laden had verbally attacked America for years, but the church was asleep. The demonic powers that were influencing him needed to be violently confronted by holy angels on assignment through the power of prayer—as in the time of Daniel.

I am certain God has raised up Nehemiahs and Esthers to do just that.

The vision of the Jerusalem Prayer Team is to have one million intercessors praying daily for national revival according to 2 Chronicles 7:14, as prophesied by King David's son, Solomon. They also emulate the prayer of King David, who declared: "Pray for the peace of Jerusalem; they shall prosper that love thee." Praying for the peace of Jerusalem is not praying for stones or dirt. They don't weep or bleed. It is praying for God's protection over the lives of the citizens of Jerusalem. It is praying for revival. It is praying for God'd grace to be poured out on the Bible land and all over the Middle East—prayer that demonic powers will be defeated by holy angels in a battle that cannot be seen with the natural eye.

The pastor of Corrie ten Boom's grandfather went to him and told him that his church was going to pray for the peace of Jerusalem. It inspired the ten Boom family to begin praying weekly. As chairman of the board of Corrie ten Boom House in Haarlem, Holland, I speak for the team when I say we have made the decision to revive this one-hundred-year-old prayer tradition. We are asking for one million Christians to join the Jerusalem Prayer Team and are asking one hundred thousand churches to begin praying weekly for the peace of Jerusalem.

Would you become a Jerusalem Prayer Team member, and would you encourage others to do so? You can email us at *jpteam@sbcglobal.net*, or write to: The Jerusalem Prayer Team,

P.O. Box 210489, Bedford, TX 76095.

The House of Israel is in a state of terror, as are all the children of the Bible land. They need the Lord to answer them in their day of terror. They need the God of Jacob to defend them. They need help from the sanctuary and strength out of Zion. Now you know my personal prayer, and when it began. I believe one million intercessors praying daily and one hundred thousand churches praying weekly for the peace of Jerusalem will move heaven and earth.

The Corrie Ten Boom House in Haarlem, Holland, is the center for the Jerusalem Prayer Team in that nation. From there, churches of all nations are being encouraged to pray for the peace of Jerusalem.

Corrie would say to the Jews in the hiding place, "Don't worry, angels are around this house. You may not see them, but they are there, protecting you." Not one Jewish person in the protection of the ten Boom Family was caught—even the ones in the hiding place escaped after the Nazis came to arrest the ten Boom family.

Over the years, a great number of Jews were hidden in the clock shop, many for just a few days as they headed for Palestine to escape Hitler's ovens. When the Gestapo (the German secret police) raided the house, the entire ten Boom family was taken prisoner.

It was the last time the ten Boom family would be together—Opa, his children, and one grandson. One hundred years before, almost to the day, in 1844, his father had started a prayer group for the "peace of Jerusalem." And now, here they were, arrested for Judenhilfe, helping Jewish people escape Nazi Persecution and death.[1]

Casper (84), Betsie (59), and Christiaan (24) died as prisoners. Corrie suffered through prison, but through a miracle, lived to tell

---

[1] *Return to the Hiding Place*, Hans Poley (Elgin, Ill: Chariot Family Publishing, 1993), 147. Mr. Poley was the first person hidden by the ten Boom family.

the story. Four Jews who were secreted in the hiding place were never caught. They miraculously escaped to safety. Even though the Nazis knew they were there, they couldn't find them.

One of the four was a Jewish rabbi who vowed he would come back and sing the praises of God. On June 28, 1942, the ten Boom family took him into their home. His name was Meijer Mossel. He was the cantor of the Jewish community in Amsterdam. He told the ten Booms, "I am a chazzen (cantor). Where is my Torah? Where is my Shul (synagogue)? Where is my congregation? The goyim (Gentiles) have laid it all to waste. They have come for the Children of Zion! My only purpose in life is to sing praises to Adonai, the Lord. I am a Yehude, a Yid (one who praises Adonai)."

In March 1974, Mossel went to Corrie ten Boom's room, and with tears of joy streaming down his face, sang to the Almighty in Hebrew. The rabbi's life had been saved through the power of prayer. As he walked downstairs, to his amazement, Corrie walked into the clock shop and stood smiling at Meijer Mossel. She had just returned from the filming of the Billy Graham movie *The Hiding Place.*

For approximately one hundred years, from 1844 to 1944, the ten Booms conducted meetings to "pray for the peace of Jerusalem." It is amazing that God would tell me eighteen years ago to restore the clock shop. To think that the Lord finally got through my thick skull that prayer, and *only* prayer, is the key.

Mother Teresa was one of the first people to tell me in Rome that she would pray daily for the Peace of Jerusalem according to Psalm 122:6. She said to me, "Love is not something you say, it's something you do." I believe that with all my heart. That is why I am appealing to you to join me in seeing what King David saw—what Soloman saw—and what our beloved Lord saw as they prayed in Jerusalem. Each experienced the power of God in Jerusalem—God's glory filled the house where they stood!

At that time Michael shall stand up,
The great prince who stands watch over the sons of your
people;
And there shall be a time of trouble,
Such as never was since there was a nation,
Even to that time.
And at that time your people shall be delivered,
Every one who is found written in the book.
And many of those who sleep in the dust of the earth shall
awake,
Some to everlasting life,
Some to shame and everlasting contempt.
Those who are wise shall shine
Like the brightness of the firmament,
And those who turn many to righteousness
Like the stars forever and ever.
But you, Daniel, shut up the words, and seal the book until
the time of the end; many shall run to and fro, and knowl-
edge shall increase.

Daniel 12:1-4 NKJV,

Behold, the nations are as a drop in a bucket,
And are counted as the small dust on the scales;. . .
All nations before Him are as nothing,
And they are counted by Him less than nothing and
worthless. . . .
Even the youths shall faint and be weary,
And the young men shall utterly fall,
But those who wait on the LORD
Shall renew their strength;
They shall mount up with wings like eagles,
They shall run and not be weary,
They shall walk and not faint.

Isaiah 40:15, 17, 30-31 NKJV

CHAPTER SIX

The Great Awakening

*As for me, I will behold Thy face in righteousness: I shall be
satisfied, when I awake, with Thy likeness.*
PSALM 17:15

When we know Jesus, are known by Jesus, and are abiding in
Jesus, we fully understand the source of our existence and the
purpose for which we were created—the hope of all our joys and
the end of all of our destinies.

Christ planned Pentecost. The inauguration of Pentecost was
even more significant than a presidential inauguration. The strategic battle plan of Pentecost was designed in heaven to transform
the world, and it did. On that day, three thousand people received
the Word and were baptized. The Bible tells us that Pentecost
"with great power gave the apostles witness of the resurrection of
the Lord Jesus: and great grace was upon them all" (Acts 4:33).

The latter-rain outpouring of God's Spirit carries the same

spiritual significance as the original (see Joel 2:23; Hosea 6:3; Zechariah 10:1; James 5:7). Multitudes will call upon the name of the Lord and be gloriously saved (see Joel 2:32; Acts 2:21, 3:19; and Romans 10:13). This mighty world revival will include the house of Israel and will amount to the greatest Jewish awakening in history (see Ezekiel 20:43–44; Jeremiah 31:34; Romans 11:24–27; Hosea 6:1–2; Amos 9:11–15; Revelation 7:1–17).

"Ask ye of the LORD *rain in the time of the latter rain"* (Zechariah 10:1), said the Old Testament prophet. Hosea 10:12 states: *"It is time to seek the* LORD, *till He come and rain righteousness upon us"* (see also Joel 2:17; Acts 1:14).

In preparation for Christ's imminent birth and ministry, God planned that the world would have interconnecting straight Roman roads and a rebuilt temple. Today He is preparing for Christ's return by procuring "a glorious church, not having spot, or wrinkle" (Ephesians 5:27), filled with powerful believers who manifest the Son's ministry on earth. The sooner we admit our spots and wrinkles, the quicker we can fuse with who He is. *Your perspective of Christ and His kingdom will determine the possibilities you pursue.*

Hosea 6:2 says that on the third day God would raise us up, and we know that a day is as a thousand years (Psalm 90:4). In this third millennium—the third thousand—we will be raised up with Resurrection power. Hosea (6:2–3) says that in the "third day" will come the "latter rain"—the last great revival before Christ's return, an unprecedented outpouring and move of the Holy Spirit more amazing than any the world has ever seen.

God is preparing us for the most momentous move in history, the one that will usher in the Lord's return. Our churches will be packed on Sundays, and believers will be tithing and enflamed for Jesus like never before. We will no longer be content with a life-style outside of the miraculous, but will be living an overcoming, victorious life in the realm of the Holy Spirit.

When Jesus begins to march, it's time for the church to move! God's last great awakening will plunder hell and populate heaven.

Jews will be included in the most massive harvest of souls in world history. Peter prophesied that there would be a mighty revival among the Jews, *times of refreshing* that would come "from the presence of the Lord" (Acts 3:19). We are going to be changed from glory to glory. The spotlight of heaven will shine on hungry hearts. Those who thirst for righteousness will be filled.

We will no longer talk about God being manifested in spurts or seasons. Ordinary believers will so fully surrender to the indwelling life of Jesus that He will gloriously reveal himself. All His prayers that have not yet been answered will be answered and manifested through us. We are about to see more than revival and more than a move of God's Spirit. *God is accelerating the application of His power for the final harvest.*

A Christian content with status-quo and business-as-usual comfort zones, living for self and bound by religious pride, will be cast aside when the Father chooses His workers for the end-time gleaning. Those who are content to live without Christ on their throne will miss the greatest heavenly power surge ever seen, empowering believers to reap the final harvest.

Compromising Christians will be devoured in the ultimate battle. The power they perceive they have will short-circuit as their dreams and visions putrefy like dead meat. *We can't limit Jesus to our timetable; we have to get on His.* God is not going to consult with us to determine His plan or purpose. It's our responsibility to determine if *we* are in *His* will, for He has made no provision to be in ours. We have not taken over the world because we have not been with Jesus. God is drawing the line and sending angels on assignments to gather saints who are hungry and thirsty for Jesus.

This move will be a manifestation of the present-day ministry of Christ. It will not be a warmed-up or heightened sense of anything we currently see or do, but a surge of the power within us—the Resurrection power that raised Jesus from the dead. Through us, it will permeate the earth.

The Big Cat

This unparalleled harvest will begin with a hunger to do the works of Jesus. Believers who are tired of faking it and tired of making excuses for not fulfilling Christ's own prophecies will commit themselves to prayer and intimacy with Him. These believers will commit themselves to and clearly see the person of the Holy Spirit. They will comprehend Christ's mission both in and through them. *These are the God-wrestlers.*

The motivation of these believers will be similar to what I experienced as Jesus appeared to me when I was eleven: clear knowledge and understanding that we have a destiny in Christ!

In general, today's Christians have no such sense of destiny. But if we find out who the Christ is within us, we will be more passionate about the Christ life than about anything the world has to offer. Such enthusiasm kills inferiority, destroys the paralysis of the past, and gives a brilliant view of an open heaven. When Christ resides in His rightful dwelling place on earth, the heavens open for those in whom He dwells.

> *When Christ resides in His rightful dwelling place on earth, the heavens open for those in whom He dwells.*

In India, my daughter wept because of a leper with no arms or legs. I asked a doctor if they could cure leprosy. He explained that most lepers don't lose their fingers and toes due to injury (they're desensitized to pain) but because they inadvertently rub them off. He said that in previous years the biggest problem was the rats chewing and eating fingers and toes when the lepers were asleep. A doctor found a cure: the cat. He tied one end of a string around the leper and the other end to a feline. When the rats came, it was the cat that ate.

We have strapped to us the Biggest Cat, the Lion of the Tribe of Judah, to consume the enemy of our souls. He is in full battle gear, and demons are trembling. He is clothed with the robe of righteousness, and his eyes are as a flame of fire. *He upholds all things by the word of His power* (see Hebrews 1:3).

When we become convinced that this Christ is in us, we will be a power that causes the enemies of the Cross to quake and cower. America's Christian youth will be an indomitable force. The cults will have nothing to offer our young people who understand *who* is abiding, dwelling, living in them.

When we're gripped with a sense of the destiny of Christ's mission and ministry, we will become caught up with seeing it operate in our lives. *What moved us in the past will not move us in the present.* We will become so enraptured with direction and destiny that we will do anything to please God.

Who on earth has a greater sense of destiny than the Lord Jesus Christ? Whose plan is greater than His? If He is going to release His present-day ministry through us, is there anything that could be more fulfilling? When we allow the Lamb of God, who takes away the sins of the world, to function through us, it will completely change our outlook.

Change Is Imminent

Staring us in the face is an eternal countdown that cannot be stopped. Every believer will have to make a choice. There will be no middle ground. *Not to choose life will result in death by default.*

To choose life is to seek after Christ with such zeal that little else matters, inviting Him to live in and through us, allowing His power to fulfill His ministry here on earth through us. *We live when we allow the life of Christ to live in and through us to fulfill His present-day ministry.*

"Their hearts will fail them for fear" is the warning for these end times. *How could Christians' hearts fail for fear?* If they haven't died to the flesh, been with Christ, and shared His sense of destiny.

The homosexuals have come out of the closet. The New

Agers, pornographers, and occult practitioners have come out of the sewer. *Now* it is time for God's blood-washed, Holy Spirit-filled children to come out of hiding and exalt Jesus as *the* King of Kings and Lord of Lords.

God is looking to see the life of His Son duplicated in our lives, to bring cataclysmic events into play through Spirit-to-spirit contact that will enable Him to send Jesus back to earth.

The King of Glory is getting ready to shake us with the present-day ministry of Jesus Christ, which will ignite a generation of unborn destinies. This power surge will overload and burn up our own ambitious plans.

No longer will the ministry of the King be determined by our futile efforts. We will make no more attempts to protect or promote our own activities; we will abdicate to the throne of heaven. The lost will then behold Christ. The Lamb of God will be made manifest in all His glory.

All heaven will move as the power reserved for the Son of God shines, blinding the powers of darkness. Armies will be subdued. The enemies of God will flee. The work of God, the final mission of the King of Glory, will be seen and felt by all.

We have been served a sandwich of Christianity between sensuality and selfishness (see Galatians 5:7). When we've been with Jesus in Spirit-to-spirit relationship, self will not enter the picture. The fullness of Christ will be manifested through us, and we can truly be a people who have been with Jesus, as the saints of old.

> *We have been served a sandwich of Christianity between sensuality and selfishness*

David, in a spiritual awakening, danced into Jerusalem with the ark of the covenant (2 Samuel 6:12–23). Elijah, in a national awakening, challenged Baal's prophets on Mount Carmel (1 Kings 18). John the Baptist declared, "Prepare ye the way of the Lord. . . . He will baptize you with the Holy Ghost, and with fire" (see Matthew 3:1–12).

We've experienced a baptism of the Holy Spirit. More than half a billion people have been baptized in the Holy Spirit. *But now we'll be baptized in fire—against such power the gates of hell cannot prevail!* We will have the white-hot fire of Christ's mission burning inside, shut up in our bones, so we can't help but speak it out, live it out.

Christ Must Have a Place to Dwell

The Bible says of the last days, "In that day will I raise up the tabernacle of David that is fallen" (Amos 9:11). Has the tabernacle of David fallen? Yes, but in far more than a physical sense. King David was dead; God wasn't speaking of him. He was speaking of Christ, *Ben David,* the son of David.

I am convinced that the tabernacle that must be rebuilt before the Second Coming is a dwelling place for Christ, *not* just a physical tabernacle. The tabernacle of David has to do with *us!* Our bodies are the dwelling place for the Spirit of Jesus. God is waiting for His children to take His Word literally and become the dwelling place—the tabernacle—for His Son.

Peter commanded at Pentecost:

> "Repent ye therefore, and be converted, that your sins may be blotted out, when the times of refreshing shall come from the presence of the Lord. And he shall send Jesus Christ, which before was preached unto you" (Acts 3:19–20).

The times of refreshing *are* coming, and Jesus himself is going to be here, residing within our tabernacles!

> ARISE [. . . to a new life]! Shine (be radiant with the glory of the Lord), for your light is come, *and the glory of the Lord is risen upon you!* For behold, darkness shall cover the earth, and dense darkness [all] peoples, but the Lord shall arise upon you. . . . And nations shall come to your

light, and kings to the brightness of your rising. (Isaiah 60:1–3 AMP, emphasis added)

The Lord appeared in an astounding vision to Isaiah and he saw the *kabod,* Christ's magnificent glory (see Isaiah 6:1–4). The angels cried "holy" as Isaiah saw the Lord sitting high and lifted up on His throne. The posts were moving, God's train was filling the temple, and smoke was pouring out. Overwhelmed, Isaiah cried,

> "Woe is me! For I am undone and ruined, because I am a man of unclean lips, and dwell in the midst of a people of unclean lips; for my eyes have seen the King, the Lord of hosts!" (6:5 AMP).

We, like Isaiah, are unclean people in an unclean society, yet the glory of the Lord is ready to rise upon us, and the nations will come to our light. *All we have to do is allow Christ to come in!*

Most of us refuse. We'll stand at the door of our lives and say, "Jesus, you can come into the living room, but don't touch anything." We keep Jesus out of the bedroom, out of the television room, out of the refrigerator, and certainly out of the kids' rooms. But He built the house! He purchased it! He is standing at the door, ready to furnish the house with every good and pleasant thing, and we're running around seeing if we can tidy up enough to allow Him to see a tiny part of it.

What are we denying Him access to when it's His dwelling place? It's like saying to the person who owns a home, "You can't come in. We can meet on the front porch, but I don't want you inside because you'll glean too much information and gain access to what I want to keep private." And it's not even ours!

Where is Christ's dwelling place going to be? We might say, "I wish someone would build that temple over there in the Middle East so the Lord can come back." *Or* we can say, "Here you are, Lord, come in and do whatever you want. I'll surrender my own thoughts about what you should do, and I'll do whatever you do, with you. *I won't hinder you!"*

> *The greatest manifestation of God's glory, power, and presence is going to hit this world through the kind of intimacy with Jesus that provides a place in which He can dwell.*

The greatest manifestation of God's glory, power, and presence is going to hit this world through the kind of intimacy with Jesus that provides a place in which He can dwell. Just as my soul has my body for its dwelling place, so Christ, by His Holy Spirit, wants my whole body and soul as completely His. Many believe that a sinner can be demon-possessed. *Yearn for the day that the world sees God's church Christ-possessed.*

Christ's Kingdom Is Coming!

Jesus said that some of those to whom He spoke wouldn't taste death until His kingdom arrived (see Mark 9:1). What did He mean? Everyone who heard Him say that died—physically. But many of them *did* see His kingdom come: they experienced the fullness of His ministry by His Spirit within themselves.

Peter saw Christ's kingdom come, and people were healed merely by having his shadow fall on them. Paul saw Christ's kingdom come, and people were healed when pieces of his clothing touched them. John saw Christ's kingdom come in the midst of a prison island, surrounded by the worst elements of society, when he was caught up in a vision of the end times, seeing Jesus in all His heavenly power. These God-wrestlers saw Christ's kingdom come in all its glory. They saw His ministry fulfilled on this earth.

We do not yet see men with the anointing that flowed in the lives of these men from the book of Acts. But do we have a vision of it? *Can we realize this is our destiny, as well?*

Western culture has softened us, causing us to settle for a comfortable what's-in-it-for-me style of Christianity rather than being willing to sacrifice for Christ and pay any price for His power and presence. Once I was in the office of a presidential candidate who had publicly proclaimed his faith in Jesus. I asked him what his political stance would be on hot issues for Christians, such as abortion.

"The way you win elections is to avoid those black-and-white issues," he responded, in effect. "Abortion is really a nonissue."

"But why?" I asked in amazement.

"Because our polls show that as many Christians have abortions as non-Christians. In fact, there is little difference in the polls between people in the church and those outside of it."

How sad. The church doesn't vote its conscience because its conscience is guilty! Politicians accordingly stay neutral, and our morality is nullified. *We haven't died to our flesh to allow Christ's holiness to be seen in our lives!*

"Holiness," in the church today, is treated as a throwback to legalistic hellfire-and-brimstone preachers. We grew tired of them because we found the life they preached impossible to attain. (Of course it was: our efforts were of the flesh.) God repeatedly says, *Ye shall be holy: for I the Lord your God am holy* (see, for example, Leviticus 11:44–45; 19:2; 20:7–26; 21:8; 22:32). Paul also issues a call to holiness (see 1 Thessalonians 4:7; 5:23). We shun holiness because we haven't attained it and mock those who claim to be holy as self-righteous bigots. We've blamed the holy life itself, when in reality it is half-crucified flesh that doesn't work.

Twenty-eight civilizations have come and gone. Myriad ministries have come and gone. Countless visions have come and gone. Innumerable people have come and gone. No matter how powerful each was in his own right, they are now gone! *Will our generation also just come and go?*

Let's get on board with what God is doing so that when He does it we're not left behind. If we as believers only do what we've always done in the next decade, we'll only have what we had in the last decade, and that is very little.

We must pray for Christ's mission to be accomplished. We're

praying for this and that and the other thing in our lives and in the lives of others. Joshua confirmed the words of Moses: *"Consecrate yourselves today to the LORD," and tomorrow God will do amazing things among you* (see Exodus 32:29). We need a pure understanding of Christ in us—the incarnational reality of the Spirit of Jesus—and prayer to complete His mission.

If we are the salt and light of the earth, why has the world taken over the church? Have we been vaccinated with a mild strain of Christianity so as to protect us from the real thing? Evangelist Ray Comfort says, "Easy salvations have provided inoculations against Christianity." Those who try to be saved without dying to the flesh will soon fall away. When the next Christian tries to connect with them and inspire them, they say, "I tried that," as if Christ were only a quit-smoking method, a medical treatment, or a trendy diet.

We preach the Cross, but for Christ's present-day ministry to operate in our lives, we must camp out at Calvary. We must invite the convicting power of the Holy Spirit into our lives and let God's house—our selves—become houses of prayer. John the Baptist said, "He must increase, but I must decrease" (John 3:30). Decreasing is not the current modus operandi of believers. We keep seeking the opposite: our visibility and enhancement through self-promotion.

Christ wants to do today what He did two thousand years ago. He has a final blow to execute. The first great battle was at Calvary. The last great battle is the end-of-the-age harvest. This is the final assault, the finished work of the Cross. This last strategic blow will render the demons of hell bound in chains and bring in the greatest harvest of souls the world has ever known.

Christ is longing and praying for us today to be intimate with Him so that He can become fully functional and fully released in us, manifesting His schedule, purposes, power, passions, and purity in order to fulfill His purpose and mission on earth. He is looking for God-wrestlers. *The battle that will allow Christ to strike*

His last great blow against His enemies is being waged right now over humankind's exalted flesh.

We are to become *"the measure of the stature of the fullness of the Christ"* (Ephesians 4:13 AMP), but we can only be this with Jesus fully functional in us.

Christ Is Sitting!

Why do most churches have small crowds at every service not held on Sunday morning? Why do four out of five Christians tithe irregularly? Why do we have to urge and plead with believers to witness to others, instead of having a compassionate life force that naturally flows from within us? Why is the prayer ministry at most churches generally the least attended of all programs?

Billions of people on earth are bound for damnation, while we spend millions and millions of dollars to strengthen the church in America. Even so, we as a church sit in pews week after week, unchanged because we do not have a vision of our true destiny in Jesus. We don't understand what the life of Christ within us can accomplish, so we fall back confidently on our fleshly works and are powerless against God's enemies. Jesus won't subjugate billions to hell while we are playing and not praying. We must gain a profound sense of the mission of Him who dwells within us.

Christ will fulfill His ministry by delegating it to us. The Pharisees didn't get it. Religious Pharisees today still don't get it. They want to box in the Holy Spirit and conduct end-time ministry in their own way. If you don't get it, you just don't get it!

Look at where Christ is now. Isaiah saw him sitting on the throne. Jesus is sitting, while billions of people desperately need to hear His voice. He's sitting, while Internet pornography plagues our homes and churches. He's sitting, while criminals fly across the world like black vultures darkening the sky, pulling children by the hundreds of thousands into sexual slavery. This Christ, who does battle against principalities and powers, is sitting! Why?

Christ is sitting because we're supposed to be standing! He has decreed and delegated the fulfillment of His ministry to us. He's sitting because He's the King, and He's waiting for us to rise up as His mighty warriors, armed and dangerous.

When you've truly been with Jesus, your passions forever change. You become a God-wrestler.

Christ has a plan to empower His bride in order to reap the final harvest. Mighty men and women will be modern-day "John the Baptists." Will you?

> *There is a world of difference between trying to live the Christian life and having Christ live His life through us.*

There is a world of difference between trying to live the Christian life and having Christ live His life through us. Religion gives us existence; Jesus gives us destiny. The flesh gives us today; the Spirit gives us eternity. In Christ, we understand the very purpose for which we were created, the hope of all of our happiness and the fulfillment of our being.

As Christ reaches through us, He speaks through us.

Men and women who have wrestled with Jesus always trigger a heavenly response to their prayers. You and I have a date with destiny. Angels are waiting for assignments. It's time we made a God-connection and allowed Him to turn on the full blast of His fire in our lives. Our families, communities, churches, and nation are hopeless without a visitation from Jesus. There is no more hope in dead religion than there is in a Hindu cow or a Buddhist temple, but there is great hope through the person of Jesus for a people who have been with Him.

God has promised He will move heaven and earth for those in hot pursuit of Him. He did just that at Calvary. A blast of eternity is shaking the earth so powerfully that even sincere believers who are trying to live the Christian life *without* surrendering control will be devastated by darkness. They will find themselves in their own sheltered bunkers, facing a roar of impotent human agony.

It's time for the mouth of hell to experience God's steel punch, administered by people who have been with Jesus. In spite of the doctrines of devils and the philosophies of fools, scoffing at the Cross and the blood, the Lord of Glory will have the final word on this planet.

Only one thing will allow Satan to disqualify us from being part of God's greatest move: refusal to dethrone self. Once we die to self, we will make a God-connection. The natural will come into contact with the supernatural, and hell will be shaken. Worry will be a thing of the past because we will see our problems from our position in Christ. We will be ruling and reigning with Him in the now. *We will be part of a Jesus generation who will not limit God.*

CHAPTER SEVEN

Smoke and Mirrors

*For now we see through a glass, darkly; but then face to face: now
I know in part; but then shall I know even as also I am known.*
1 CORINTHIANS 13:12

The pathway to revival is clearly marked: it always starts by
admitting what we are not. At first, John Kilpatrick's congregation
loved the changes that made their church grow to a size only 1
percent of America's churches could boast. By most standards of
measurement, John was a tremendous success; nevertheless, he
was miserable because he was honest enough to admit that he
wasn't in the presence of Jesus—that Jesus was not living His life
through him.

*It's one thing to be willing to say a prayer, but another to become
a living prayer. Making a sacrifice is wonderful, but becoming a
sacrifice . . . that is Christlike.* We often believe making a small
sacrifice for Jesus covers our bases, refusing to offer our lives as

living sacrifices by placing them on the altar of God. John laid it all down, admitting what was *not* happening in his life and ministry.

Genesis 32:28 says of Jacob: "Thy name shall be called no more Jacob, but Israel: for as a prince hast thou power with God and with men, and hast prevailed." Most in the church today act like paupers instead of princes!

This Power Is Available to Believers Today

The kiss of God, releasing His glory through the person of the Holy Spirit, is for ordinary people, for every believer, for anyone who wants to come close enough to receive it.

Jesus prayed through an ordinary Christian named Si Rickman, echoed by a humble woman of God, saving our lives. I was flying in a private Cessna with friends Paul Cole, Si Rickman, and our pilot; the engine started to break apart, causing a vibration so disruptive the fuel line broke loose. It was 11:25 P.M., and Si Rickman, a Christian layman, started praying: *"Angels of the Lord, undergird us."* For thirty minutes he prayed, while Paul Cole held a flashlight to the instrument panel, and we lost two thousand feet of altitude against a fifty-mile-per-hour headwind. Yet at 11:55 P.M. that same night we landed safely at an airport. In no way should we have made it.

The next morning a praying saint by the name of Opal Weeks called my office and said, "The Holy Spirit woke me at 11:25 last night and told me to pray for thirty minutes that the angels of the Lord would undergird you. Are you okay?"

God can anoint ordinary believers and manifest the present-day ministry of Christ. And He will, if you wrestle with Him.

The world is groaning for the manifestation of Jesus. He *will* reveal himself through a people who have been with Him and wrestled in prayer.

It will be a wonderful day when we are caught up with Jesus Christ in the clouds of glory. Yet 1 John 3:2, which describes this event, may have a dual interpretation, now *and* then. God is going to so fill us with His presence and power that we will truly know Him. He will manifest himself in us, and we will see Him as He is and be like Him. *Changed from glory to glory, we will be a people who have been with Jesus.*

We Need to Detox!

I loved doing the talk-show circuit: *Good Morning America, Nightline, Regis and Kathie Lee, Geraldo, Crossfire* . . . boy, was it fun being a "Christian celebrity." I truly thought I was a Holy Spirit atomic bomb, when there wasn't enough power in my life to blow up a piggy bank!

Precious saints put up with my pathetic preaching and off-key singing, their hearts breaking with the sound of my laborious sermons, because they only hoped for a touch of Jesus—I was too full of myself to get low with Him. There wasn't enough anointing on me to heal a mosquito. I needed to detoxify, to flush my system clean from the pollutants I'd so happily ingested. *I couldn't understand why more souls weren't being saved in "my" ministry. I couldn't understand why I didn't have joy and peace.* I thought it was because I was carrying such heavy burdens, but the true cause was spiritual barrenness, testifying against me. My agitation, ease of offense, and insensitivity to those around me were the result of barrenness: the fruit of *not* being with Jesus.

Ministering isn't about the White House or television. It's always been about being with Jesus.

Beyond Spiritual "Success"

Prayer alone doesn't mean you've been with Jesus. Muslims pray and Hindus pray. You can be sincere and religious, praying repeatedly, and still not be with Jesus. You can read your Bible until you wear out the pages and still not be with Jesus. *Do you want to be with Jesus? Do you realize what is hindering you from being with Jesus?* If you are willing to pay the price, God is going to show up in a manner that will exceed your comprehension.

In Saudi Arabia, as I returned to the Gulf Meridian Hotel, covered with dirt, I saw six Kuwaiti princes. As they glanced toward me, Jesus spoke softly to my spirit: *"Go to them."* I walked over, and before I realized what was happening, I started to prophesy: "Thus saith the Lord Jesus of Nazareth, who shed His blood on the Cross of Calvary, and has been praying for you and your country. He will give you your country back. It will happen very quickly with hardly any of your people being killed."

The Kuwaitis looked at me with wide eyes, and one asked, "Are you a prophet of God?"

Another said, "We think you are."

"No," I said, "I'm not a prophet."

"Yes, we think you are," one insisted, "and if this prophecy comes to pass, we will invite you to Kuwait to speak to us and the royal family about this Jesus and His cross."

As I left to find my room, tears streamed down my face, and I understood how mighty our lives could be if we only let Christ live *His* life through ours. Sending me forth when I was weak from surgery, Jesus kissed me with His strength in the Middle East. We cannot wrestle with God without influencing the lives of those around us, drawing them closer to Jesus.

Such experiences have not dominated my life, but have come in isolated instances. Self stands in the way, demanding to be in control. I pray by the grace of God that our lives might become perpetually living manifestations of Jesus and not merely rare experiences with a seasonal blast of His glory. *It's not about me; it's about Him!*

We need to become so hungry and thirsty for the present-day ministry of Christ that we'll move beyond the quest for spiritual "success." We must have such zeal for the fulfillment of His mission that we'll do whatever it takes to get into that heavenly Holy Spirit zone, the Holy of Holies, until the breakthrough comes.

The apostle John saw victorious believers as kings and priests, reigning on the earth (see Revelation 5:10). The Old Testament says that in the spring of the year, the kings went to battle. When are the kings who rule and reign with Christ going to fight the war? What is the time of our battle cry?

I see individual hearts today set ablaze: Coming together in unity, forming a mighty army, consumed with the fire of God, ready to complete Christ's mission, defeating His enemies.

Pastor David Wilkerson, well known for his prophetic ministry over the years, has said of the Pensacola revival, "This is not that." He said if the sporadic revivals we've seen were the final great awakening, all the cities of America would be shaken. *That's what's coming next*—the revolutionizing of cities and entire nations! Pensacola is the first fruit, but we're going *beyond*!

Christ is blowing the shofar to call us into battle. It's now the spring of the year. *God has raised up His church as kings and priests to go out to battle, not in our power, but in His.*

We Can Shake and Bake, or We Can Break Before God

Many years ago I was invited to speak at a youth conference, along with some prominent youth evangelists. As we prayed together before the meeting, one of the organizers said, "Please tell us what God is saying will happen here." Each of the speakers spoke up quickly, almost flippantly, as though altering an eternal destiny or the fervency of a nation were the simplest task. "This conference will change the destiny of America," someone said. "There will be an outpouring that will shake these kids."

I volunteered nothing until they asked me. Even back then, I knew something was terribly wrong with the picture we were painting. I was crying as I said, "God has told me nothing. The only thing I see are tens of thousands of young people who are not mighty warriors. They have been mentored by all the shuck and jive, shake and bake, smoke and mirrors theatrics we represent. My prayer for this meeting is that the tent will fall, the microphones will short out, and God will shame us into being broken before Him, so they will see only Christ, and we would not use this to build our own kingdoms."

When we acknowledge the "great omission"—confessing that we've been following the self life instead of the Christ life—only then will we feel the impact of the Great Commission.

We must pray that the mountains constructed by fleshly pursuits come down, so the valleys of our lives can be filled with God's glory. We must want to be filled with fresh oil and fresh fire! Our cry must be to please only the Father. We must lay down everything that hinders us from that objective. *Our hearts must bleed for souls until our only cry is for more of God.*

> *We must pray that the mountains constructed by fleshly pursuits come down, so the valleys of our lives can be filled with God's glory.*

Surrendering our lives to the King of Glory closes the mouth of hell and opens the window of heaven. The Lion of Judah has been sent to roar through those who have broken hearts or broken wings.

"Then had the churches rest throughout all Judaea and Galilee and Samaria, and were edified; and walking in the fear of the Lord, and in the comfort of the Holy Ghost, were multiplied" (Acts 9:31). *Encouragement, edification, comfort, and a harvest of souls come when we see flesh through God's eternal perspective.* We need a fresh revelation of the Father. When we look at Him through the revelation of eternity, we will fear the Lord.

God is raising up an army of believers who will live in the light of eternity rather than in lust or bondage, not being defeated and dominated by sin, and not attempting to cover up our wrongs with the hypocrisy that causes a lost and dying world to mock rather than to fall on their knees, weeping and crying, and wanting to touch the hem of Jesus' garment.

We Must Release the Kingdom of God Within

The Christian life is to be lived in the Spirit, not the flesh. We must crucify the flesh, mortifying its members, and die to self so that the Spirit of God can rule and reign in our lives. The Bible says it's like a seed that falls into the ground and dies only to spring up. Jesus said that the hour had come for the Son of Man to die (see John 12): *He* is our example.

"We have this treasure in earthen vessels, that the excellency of the power may be of God, and not of us" (2 Corinthians 4:7). We have to remember the power is from God and is *inside* the clay jar (see NIV), not outside. God literally placed the person of Jesus, through the Holy Spirit, in our earthen vessels! Only when our external flesh is broken can the power of the treasure's aroma be received into heaven.

I once accompanied Jamie Buckingham, the late Christian journalist, to the Sinai Desert. We were to climb the mountain where Moses became weary during battle and Aaron and Hur held up his hands. I took off my shirt and two canteens and jogged up the mountain because I didn't want to walk as slowly as the rest of the group. By the time I reached the top, I had heatstroke. I was sick, but too proud to tell them. That night as I cleaned our pots and pans with sand, every cell in my body screamed in agony. I was deeply upset that I'd been so foolish as to jog in the desert. When I finally crawled into my sleeping bag, Jesus gently asked, *"Why did it happen?"*

"Because the men wouldn't move fast enough," I replied.
"Why did it happen?"
"Because I took my shirt off."
"Why did it happen?"
"Because I took my canteens off."
"Why did it happen?"
"Because I jogged too fast."
"Why did it happen?"
I finally broke. "Lord, it happened because I was stubborn,

self-willed, and filled with pride; and I humble myself and repent."

When through tears I uttered these words, God's power instantly healed me. I shined my flashlight down on my open Bible. It said the children of Israel were murmuring and complaining, even as God had provided food for nourishment and brought victory in battle (see Exodus 17). *Here I was in the same exact spot, doing the same exact thing.*

The next day as we passed a tent, a mother came running out. Earlier her little girl had fallen headfirst into the cooking fire. Her hair was burned off, she had a terrible infection that was matted with flies, and she was burning up with fever. Her parents' only medical knowledge was to heat knives and burn the flesh to kill the infection, scarring the child for life. Jesus instructed me to place my hand on the green oozing infection and pray. That night we traveled a considerable distance. The next afternoon a doctor traveling with us said, "I have to go back and operate on that child. I'm afraid she might not make it." We all returned with him.

Shortly after we arrived, I could hear the doctor crying in the tent. I thought he'd been operating, but he hadn't—he was being operated *on!* As I opened the tent flap, I saw why he wept. The mother was rocking the little girl, whose head was totally pink, with no sign of infection and no scars. The child had been miraculously and completely healed! *The honor we wrestle for is His honor.*

Jesus had taken me to the point of brokenness so He could lead me on a divine appointment in which He could touch and heal this little girl. He was looking for a vessel that would yield so He could operate through it. *Dear saints, we are the vessels that God has chosen, the vessels through which He wants to operate, the vessels He seeks to use for the manifestation of His glory in the end times.*

Every time God has kissed me it has come at a time of total brokenness in my life. We don't have to be shattered by external forces. We can humble ourselves and be used by God.

Like the jar of precious nard broken to anoint Jesus, there has to be brokenness in order for Jesus, the perfume of God, to flow out. The flesh treasures a powerless religious vessel because the flesh emphasizes the outside, not the inside. As long as we experience some form of success through our own strength, we will continue to cling to the jar, the shell, the outer man.

Author Tommy Tenney said, *"There can be no openness in heaven before there is brokenness on earth."*

We cannot afford any longer to underestimate or undervalue this incredible, unearthly stratagem: Christ himself became for us a broken vessel in the flesh, and the glory that poured forth changed the world by releasing the person of the Holy Spirit into our lives. When our earthly vessels are broken before God, the life of Christ is released, which *will* bring a heavenly response.

God's Goal Is to Exhaust Us

After hearing sermons, sometimes my own, I've come away with a new set of baggage to unload or a new set of instructions to follow. I feel the condemnation of not doing it right, so I pull myself up, grit my teeth, and try harder. But God wants me to cease from my labors, lay down my life, and become resurrected with the life of Jesus. That's when Christ's burden becomes light and His yoke easy. I now see that God's goal is to exhaust my efforts; He knows He cannot empower me when self is in control of my life.

Dr. Cho once advised me, "You must empty yourself." Every time a person has been emptied to become totally dependent upon Christ, the earth has been shaken. It shook for David Livingstone. It shook for William Seymour. It shook for Charles Finney. It shook for John Kilpatrick. The Lord knows, as does Satan, that when the glory of the Father is manifested through us, it will shake this earth.

The world is waiting for sanctified Christians, emptied of

flesh, to rise up with the power of the living God. *Why don't we see the mighty miracles of faith today? Because we are not broken!*

After thirty years of partnering with thousands of pastors from all over the world, believing God with them for revival in their churches, cities, and nations, I believe that *revival is not transmittable*. It can't be caught like the flu. Pentecost will not spread like an epidemic.

We tend to believe that what God does is dependent on what we do: how we preach, how many songs we sing, and how much time we spend in prayer. We short-circuit His purposes because we don't admit what we're not. We don't understand that the manifestation of Jesus is not about *our* ministry but about *His*.

People can sing the same songs, duplicate similar messages, and advertise another move of the Spirit, but no one can "catch" revival. You can preach in the flesh and sing in the flesh, but *one thing you cannot do in the flesh is be with Jesus: There is a price to pay.* John and Brenda Kilpatrick paid the price by dying to their flesh and pressing into God's presence for two-and-a-half years before the Holy Spirit manifested Christ's ministry in Pensacola.

Christ will never manifest himself with power and glory through the believer if the focus is on the promotion of self, the building of an organization, or the finding of "new ideas." When believers are gossiping, competing, judging, scheming, manipulating, and bragging, there will be no revival. When we smugly denounce one another and demand that everyone else repent, we can be sure the flesh is alive, the person of the Holy Spirit is grieved, and genuine revival is on a fast track to the graveyard.

The cycle of self is perpetuated by a Christian system that has convinced us that our life is all about our selves and getting more of God into our self. Today, what hinders God-visitation (genuine revival) is not divorce, drugs, or pornography; again, the *primary* obstacle is an unwillingness to die to self, to reject a theology that empowers religious flesh. It's not about our bragging about how much we have of God. The decadent condition of our nation reveals how much we open ourselves to God—we are to be its light and salt. *The real issue is how much God has of us.*

> *The cycle of self is perpetuated by a Christian system that has convinced us that our life is all about our selves and getting more of God into our self.*

There is a world of difference between seeking improvement through our flesh and pursuing the presence of God in the Spirit; between having a good service and experiencing a move of God; between a rude awakening and the great awakening.

The Father's intention is that we completely surrender so He can fill us with the fullness of the Son until we are 100 percent convinced we will fail without Him.

Jesus Is Coming in the Now

Jesus is coming! We enthusiastically sing it. We dynamically preach it. We devotedly teach it. But does it make a difference in our lives *now*? Yes, Jesus is coming on the clouds one day. But He is coming within the believer's life *now*. Jesus' own unanswered prayers—"Greater things will you do" and "Thy will be done on earth"—reveal that He is not only coming *someday*. The full, unhindered flow of His Spirit is ready now to pour out of those who press in to be with Him. The Spirit of God wants to make contact with our spirits so there can be a heavenly ignition, manifesting the face of Jesus *in us and through us* in our daily lives.

Think of who truly had the right to be mentioned in the Bible. No one but Jesus. Every biblical man and woman of God is there because of Jesus. He is found in the Bible from start to finish. Consider some of those He visited:

Abraham, the idol-worshiper from a long line of idol-worshipers, saw Christ as he sacrificed to Him by faith.

Moses, the wanted murderer, running for his life, saw Christ in a burning bush.

Jacob, the con artist, wrestled Christ.

Gideon, the coward, was visited by Christ and was declared a mighty man of valor.

Peter, whose denial was forgiven, was loved and taught by Christ.

Paul, the Christian-killing hypocrite of all hypocrites, saw Christ revealed to him on the road to Damascus.

Each of these men received the kiss of God after they had been with Jesus. But what they saw, felt, heard, and experienced—the magnificent works of God performed in and through them—can never compare to what this final generation will taste in Christ.

> *One day, fully surrendered to the purposes of God, we will render more fruit than a lifetime of good intentions.*

Christ has destined for us a magnificent heritage, greater than the inheritance of Abraham. But the resurrected life can only be inherited if we admit what we are not. *We cannot live until we learn how to die.*

Former President Ronald Reagan had a sign on his desk that read,

> *A man can become too big in his own eyes to be used by God, but never too small in his own eyes.*

We need to get small in our own eyes. After a recent Texas tornado, prayer warriors in a prayer tower that was directly hit said they survived by getting flat on their faces. When they stood up, they could see the city. We need to get low with Jesus so we can rise up and see things from His eternal perspective.

One day, fully surrendered to the purposes of God, we will render more fruit than a lifetime of good intentions. The present-day ministry of Jesus Christ operating through your life and mine will bring about a God-visitation to transform a lost and dying world. This mighty move is going to be so unfathomable that people will start seeing the church house as a birth house because of the phenomenal number of new births that will take place there. *Staffed by ordinary Christians, the church will be a "Holy Spirit baby factory" for new creatures in Christ.*

CHAPTER EIGHT

Living Flesh Is Deadly

[I am] confident of this very thing, that he which hath begun a
good work in you will perform it until the day of Jesus Christ.
PHILIPPIANS 1:6

While serving as a medic in the military, part of my job was to
treat patients with facial injuries. I had the choice of using a butterfly Band-Aid, suturing the wound with fine needles, or debrid-
ing it. In the debridement process, a saline solution would be
injected under the skin of the patient's inner arm, similar to the
size area of the scarring on his face. This caused the skin to be
elevated so it could be cut. Then I would literally place the trans-
plant onto the patient's face, and the new skin would graft onto
the injured area.

In wrestling with God, we literally take the supernatural life
of Christ, impose it on our own, and allow His life to take over
our tainted flesh. The world's entertainment, lusts, and distractions

that contaminate Christians are "reverse debridement," where a section of bad flesh has been placed over the desire for righteousness, and we have incorporated it into our lives, thinking it normal.

> *In wrestling with God, we literally take the supernatural life of Christ, impose it on our own, and allow His life to take over our tainted flesh.*

The cure for bad flesh is not to cut off the infected or injured piece. It cannot be cleaned up or covered over with makeup. A butterfly bandage doesn't cure a life-threatening illness. The antidote to the world's pollution and our failing flesh is to strap ourselves to Christ until we truly become one!

For this cause shall a man leave his father and mother, and shall be joined unto his wife, and they two shall be one flesh. This is a great mystery: but I speak concerning Christ and the church. (Ephesians 5:31–32)

Paul described marriage as a mystery in which two become "one flesh." Marriage is an illustration of the dynamic fusion that occurs between Jesus and us, a joining that releases the supernatural into our lives. Paul said he was persuaded that *nothing can separate the church from the love of God in Christ Jesus* (see Romans 8:39).

When self is off the throne, *we will know the Holy Spirit* not simply as a gift or an encouragement but *in the person of Jesus Christ*. Then the impossible becomes possible, our unanswered prayers are answered, and we are released to do the "greater works"!

We are coming face to face with Christ, as Jacob did at Peniel. This was foreshadowed also in the life of Elijah. A friend of Elijah's gave birth to a son after he prophesied over her. Years later the child died, so she called for Elijah. He sent his servant ahead with his staff; three times the servant laid Elijah's staff on the child, but the boy remained dead. When Elijah finally arrived, he stretched his body on top of the child—eye to eye, mouth to mouth, and hand to hand—and cried out three times to God. The Lord's anointing came into that child, who instantly returned to life. The life of Christ, anchored to us, resuscitates our decaying flesh the same way Elijah's life worked on the dead boy. *Wrestling with God is a matter of life and death.*

Jesus wants to meet us eye to eye and hand to hand, breathing the breath of life into us. When our flesh dies at the Cross, our spirit can live in resurrection.

Some years ago, Jesus softly directed me to invite a dozen men to join me in Jerusalem; He said we would affect the destiny of Israel. I had no idea what the Lord was going to do. The night I arrived, God gave me a vision and said that what He was going to do was none of my business; it was *His*. During the next few days we prayed over the prime minister; I had all the men in the room hold hands together with him as we prayed. His army general had a toothache and asked for prayer as we were walking out the door.

Soon after I returned home, I was awakened by a telephone call from Dr. Reuben Hecht, the senior advisor to the prime minister of Israel. "God has answered your prayers," he said. "We have shot down ninety Russian MiGs and twenty-five hundred SAM missiles without losing one plane." The Lebanese War had broken out immediately after we left! God had sent us, by the person of the Holy Spirit, to minister and to pray.

This is how the life of Christ manifests His power through us— in obedience.

Crucified Flesh

The crucified man is not a popular theme because it's the greatest threat to Satan's kingdom. Satan has tried to blind the eyes of believers from understanding what it means to be crucified with Christ. Crucifying the flesh means acknowledging we cannot please God in our flesh. If the apostle Paul had to die daily to his flesh, why do we propagate a contrary theology?

> *If the apostle Paul had to die daily to his flesh, why do we propagate a contrary theology?*

As long as we depend upon our flesh, we're bankrupt and helpless. When we see flesh through the eyes of eternity, the righteous Spirit of the Lord begins to increase in us. Then He shows us things to come, the riches of Christ in glory, His keeping power, His light, and His wisdom.

The Holy Spirit glorifies Christ. "He shall glorify me: for he shall receive of mine, and shall shew it unto you" (John 16:14). The person of the Holy Spirit delivers to believers all that the Father has given His Son (see v. 15).

Since the Spirit of Christ dwells in the believer, we must surrender our unholy flesh for Him to blast through us with glory. *He cannot resurrect living flesh.*

His power and our inability meet in Spirit-to-spirit contact, and the same Spirit that resurrected Christ gives us life.

> If the Spirit of him that raised up Jesus from the dead dwell in you, he that raised up Christ from the dead shall also quicken your mortal bodies by his Spirit that dwelleth in you. (Romans 8:11)

Paul became a dead man speaking and seeing through the eyes of eternity to dead men and women. The less we die to our flesh, the less we know Jesus. He asked His disciples if they were able to be baptized with His baptism, for it is a baptism of suffering. Dying to the flesh hurts.

Our flesh, like water, follows the course of least resistance. Before we came to Jesus, our flesh ruled us. However, through the fellowship of His suffering, Christ has made a way to exchange our mortality with His immortality, our imperfection with His perfection. *We can sit with Christ if we are willing to suffer with Him* (see Hebrews 2:10).

After I emptied myself of all the unimpressive posturing, plotting, and politicking of a supposed "big-time evangelist," the Lord impressed upon my heart that I was to partake of the *fellowship of His sufferings* (see Philippians 3:10). *Oh no, I thought. Not more suffering. Not after what I lived through as a boy.* But I've learned that suffering is humbly surrendering our self life to the Christ life.

I started in ministry at age nineteen in Philadelphia, with three dollars and some change. My clothes and wallet had been stolen. My car had broken down. I had walked miles in the snow from a church to a diner, and now, as I sat eating, extremely discouraged, Jesus whispered, *"Son, your eyes have not seen, your ears have not heard, and it has not been revealed to your spirit the things that I have prepared for you, but I will reveal them unto you by the Holy Spirit."*

When we operate in the power of His resurrection, God takes us from hopelessness into a state of vitality, restoring our destiny. He is prophetically declaring resurrection for us, to fill us with power and glory, no matter how hopeless we may feel.

Without Resurrection power, everything seems impossible. We quit on our marriages, finances, children, ministries, churches, careers, and relationships. We dump visions and dreams, becoming "betrayers" (see Acts 7:51–52). We pronounce death over everything *except* the flesh!

Jesus lived in the flesh to conquer it and let us know it can be conquered through Him. He declared, "My meat is to do the will of him that sent me, and to finish his work" (John 4:34). Jesus never had a smaller portion of the Holy Spirit: He was filled with the fullness, and He declares that we will be also (see Ephesians 4:13). A Christian who has evicted the flesh and stripped it of all of its rights and privileges will have the power of the Holy Spirit without measure (see Ephesians 1:18–19).

Jesus prayed, "And now, O Father, glorify thou me with thine own self with the glory which I had with thee before the world was" (John 17:5). He asked the Father to keep His disciples safe from evil (John 17:15). As the flesh is crucified, through the power of the Holy Spirit, we are kept from the evil one. We are sanctified through the truth, made pure and holy.

Second Trip to the Cross

Paul said he died *daily* (1 Corinthians 15:31). Believers grieve the heart of God when they refuse to continually die to self. *Most of us have never taken a second trip to the cross.* We went the first time to surrender and confess the sins that were condemning our souls. We sing about the cross, talk about the cross, but rarely return to the foot of the cross to lift up Jesus. *In essence, anything less is nailing Christ to the cross afresh.* For believers, relegating the cross to Easter musicals and Sunday melodies is a blatant defiance of the power of His blood.

The Father is looking for Christians who are willing to pay any price, refusing to promote personalities over the person of Jesus Christ, not accepting the starvation of the sheep.

When we allow Christ to lead us to the Cross and draw us to our knees, He communicates with us . . . and the finger of a mighty God will touch the soul of a lowly, needy human being.

Since our flesh is not holy, we have to daily bring it under subjection to the person of the Holy Spirit in order to become alive in Christ. Paul shook the world, yet every day he acknowledged everything he was not. Every day he admitted that if he acted in the flesh he could never see anything close to the results God would gain from the same amount of effort in the Spirit.

We cannot live by the wits of our flesh in hopes of outsmarting the devil. The Holy Spirit doesn't run around the globe helping believers come up with new ideas to live the Christian life. He is pointing us back to the original idea, the present-day ministry of Jesus Christ manifesting himself in the now, just as powerfully as He did two thousand years ago, through the believer, with a divine schedule.

Remember: *Believers grieve the Holy Spirit by attempting to live for Christ without dying to their flesh.* Repentance is not just an act for sinners and backsliders; repentance is a daily bath of Christ's blood for every praying believer. *God, forgive us for the things that hinder you!*

When we resist Christ, we grieve Him. The problem is, we don't want to bow. If we don't serve an earthly king, it is difficult for us to understand that we do serve a heavenly king. The Bible says *every* knee will bow, and *every* tongue will ultimately confess that Jesus Christ is Lord (see Philippians 2:10–11). When we resist the person of the Holy Spirit, we're resisting Christ, grieving the One who is making intercession for us.

Paul was once proud of his religious flesh, which was a stench in the nostrils of God. Eventually, he learned to count his flesh as *dung* (Philippians 3:8). Our flesh is certainly no better than his, yet we smear ourselves in dung and get applauded by others as we roll around in it more and more. *This is why the world has not seen Jesus.*

God promised that He would pour out His Spirit on all flesh (see Joel 2:28). Jesus paid the inconceivable price to fulfill this promise. *God sent His only Son in sinful flesh that we might live in the Spirit:*

> For what the law could not do, in that it was weak through the flesh, God sending his own Son in the likeness of sinful flesh, and for sin, condemned sin in the flesh: that the righteousness of the law might be fulfilled in us, who walk not after the flesh, but after the Spirit. For they that are after the flesh do mind the things of the flesh; but they that are after the Spirit the things of the Spirit. . . . So then *they that are in the flesh cannot please God.* But ye are not in the flesh, but in the Spirit, if so be that the Spirit of God dwell in you. (Romans 8:3–5, 8–9, emphasis added)

The present-day ministry of Jesus is not about Christians *living* with Christ. It's about Christians *dying* with Christ. There are no negatives in dying to self; we will never be penalized for it.

Last New Year's Eve I was asked about my resolutions for the upcoming year. My response was *"I am resolving to learn how to die."* Only when we are willing to die to ourselves will Christ fully live in us. This is the challenge to all who wrestle with God. *Are you willing?*

Wanted: Dead Men

Christians routinely go through baptism rituals without deeply recognizing the significance of it. We repent for the minor guilt we feel, but we don't deal with the root cause. In the sense that baptism is symbolic of a funeral, Christian funerals are often performed decades late! We're better off writing our own obituary, signing it, and dating it the day we died to our flesh. *That's the day we truly entered eternal life.*

My abusive father tithed, attended church, and apparently was even close to his pastor. But he beat me and my brother and sister with belts and coat hangers for senseless reasons. He belted me, battered me, and berated me. He once choked me with an extension cord and left me for dead, lying on the bedroom floor with my face in my vomit. He beat my mother many Friday nights and sometimes in between. Meanwhile, he impregnated other women, having no conscience about it. He would get drunk at the Twilight Café most Saturday nights, then get up on Sunday morning to sing at church. My father had the Ten Commandments printed on the back of his business cards, and he persisted in breaking almost every one of them.

When I was eleven and Jesus entered my room, the encounter was so powerful it became my most private secret. No one knew until I was thirty-two.

At age nineteen, I finally told my mother that I was going to follow Jesus. She coldly replied, "This is the worst day of my life. I'd rather you told me you were gay or a drug addict. We would go buy a coffin for you and hold your funeral, because you would be dead to us."

The thought thrilled me. Not realizing how much I would hurt her feelings, I responded cheerfully, "Mom, that's great! I wish you would do it!"

The pronouncement of my death sounded like the best thing that could ever happen to me. Yet, like most of us, instead of completely dying to the flesh when I was born again, I dragged my flesh around year after year. Whenever I've fed the self life, my death has been prolonged and my obituary has sadly lengthened.

The goal is for our obituary to grow more slowly each year until it finally stops. *The best (and most accurate) earthly tombstone epitaph contains the date of our conversion to Christ.*

But the flesh goes absolutely insane with rage, kicking and screaming, determined that it will not be crucified with Christ. *Being crucified with Jesus is absolute nonsense!* it wails; *Christ was crucified, that's good enough!* Many Christians pray for more power and more faith, but they don't realize that as long as self is on the throne, they are praying for power to empower their own flesh. This is all flesh, and the sooner we end it by writing our own obituary, the better off the world will be!

When we become drunk with power, drunk with prestige, drunk with flesh, we fail to acknowledge who God truly is. *God is against flesh, because flesh is against God.* Anytime we say, "I have arrived" or "I did this great thing," refusing to acknowledge God's grace in our lives, we have rent ourselves away from the hem of His garment of grace and have flown off into the oblivion of fleshly endeavors.

The Holy Spirit is bringing us to our own death, to our own funeral, so we can write our own obituary. We must no longer try to use Him as some type of Super-Vitamin to give us the power and determination to be strong, using the Word of God, our faith, and our prayers to attempt to get our flesh to do what's right.

God is looking for dead men who desire to know nothing except the power of the Resurrection, whose banner is *"Not by might, nor by power, but by my spirit, saith the* LORD *of hosts"*

(Zechariah 4:6). He will subdue and conquer all our sins by the power of the Holy Spirit. We must comprehend the glorious revelation that the same Jesus who has purified our soul can purge our flesh: "If ye through the Spirit do mortify the deeds of the body [the flesh], ye shall live" (Romans 8:13).

Do Bad Things Happen to Good People?

If our flesh falls on Christ, the Rock, we're saved. If the Rock falls on us, we're crushed. It's always easier to voluntarily die to our flesh than to have it exposed to the world. Preachers learn it is always easier to die *before* a message than after. It is always easier to die in private than in public.

Sometimes, though, for our flesh to die, we must be arrested in our flesh and stopped cold in our tracks so that Resurrection power can save us from a path of destruction. In such cases, our earthly view of what is "bad" obscures the truth. We don't always need "bad" things to happen to us, but we do have to die to our flesh. Depending on how hardheaded or hardhearted we are, bad things are actually good when they cause our flesh to die.

Do bad things happen to good people? Yes: *They succeed in their flesh!* That's the worst-case scenario—accomplishing something we can attribute to our fleshly abilities. Dying to our flesh, by contrast, is the best thing that could ever happen to us. Certainly this was what happened with me when everything I'd ever built came crashing down around me, showing me the opportunity to die and be resurrected with Christ.

The Bible explicitly tells us to rejoice in the midst of trials:

> Beloved, do not be surprised at the fiery ordeal that is taking place among you to test you, as though something strange were happening to you. But rejoice insofar as you are sharing Christ's sufferings, so that you may also be glad and shout for joy when his glory is revealed. If you are reviled for the name of Christ, you are blessed, because the spirit of glory, which is the Spirit of God, is resting on you.

But let none of you suffer as a murderer, a thief, a criminal, or even as a mischief maker. Yet if any of you suffers as a Christian, do not consider it a disgrace, but glorify God because you bear this name. (1 Peter 4:12–16 NRSV)

My brothers and sisters, whenever you face trials of any kind, consider it nothing but joy. (James 1:2 NRSV)

It is a joyous occasion when God, in His mercy and love, stops us from being our fleshly selves. We wallow and complain, "I can't believe this is happening to me!" We worry our friends with "what we are going through." That's not the point. *When we surrender completely to Christ, we will see what we are going to—Christ and all of His glory!*

We must embrace joy whenever we have an opportunity to die to more of our flesh. We can give thanks in everything because of our trust that God will never do anything to hurt us, but only help us (see 1 Thessalonians 5:18).

We read things like "Bless them which persecute you: bless, and curse not" (Romans 12:14). If the flesh is dead, those who curse us are only cursing our flesh . . . which is cursed and dead already.

When self is on the throne of your life, you can be sure chaos will be the norm, no matter how religious you are. *Chaos is a sure sign that you are not abiding in Jesus.* A chaotic Christ couldn't heal a broken heart.

> *When self is on the throne of your life, you can be sure chaos will be the norm, no matter how religious you are.*

Our Fleshprints or His Footprints?

Before Christ can shake the world through us, we must allow Him to shake the flesh out of us. We cannot follow both Jesus and the flesh, but we can die to our flesh and become alive in the Spirit. A flesh-fed world can never see the living Christ through a flesh-fed Christian.

I remember going on a hunt and wounding a wild boar. I needed my dog to track him, but the boar went into the muddy creek where many other tracks and scents confused my dog. Every boar had the same scent. The key was to go back to the blood trail, which my dog was able to follow easily, so I could bag the boar.

In a reverse way, we all have fleshprints that smell of flesh, easy for a demon to hunt down for the kill. When we reek of flesh, we don't scare demons, no matter how much or how loudly we pray. But those demon powers can distinguish traces of blood. When we have the scent of the blood of Jesus on us, because we have been wrestling with God, demons pick up the scent and stay off that trail. When we are covered in the blood of Jesus, they avoid us the same way they avoid the presence of God. They'd rather go down to the muddy creek bed and fight with all the flesh they smell wallowing around there!

In the Greek, one definition of *bema* is "footprints." Scripture tells us that *the church will go before the "bema" seat of God, where we will be judged for how closely we have walked in the footprints of Jesus.* Christ has created bloodied footprints for us. When we die to our flesh and become alive to the Spirit, we are led by Him, which causes our footprints to match Christ's. The trail we then leave is the blood trail of the footprints of Jesus. The blood trail of Jesus causes demons to tremble and the world to shake.

If you're bound by flesh, you must go back to the blood trail where the blood of Christ was applied.

Walking in the Supernatural

Paul said, "Make not provision for the flesh" (Romans 13:14) because "no flesh should glory in His presence" (1 Corinthians 1:29). I used to read such passages and think, *I'm not doing the "big sins,"* so *I'm not in the flesh.* I didn't realize how much the flesh clung to me!

From the time I met Jesus face to face when I was eleven, I

had learned to cry out to Him, "Help me, Lord!" The night Jesus visited me was the greatest of my life. I was gloriously born again. The storms in my home raged on, but Christ had calmed me in the midst of the tumult.

About ten years later I entered the ministry, very aware that just about every other minister was more talented, more intelligent, and more educated than I was. I cried out to God, "I'm not able in my own strength; please help me!" I knew I didn't have the gifts or abilities to do virtually anything I was being called to do, and yet the amazing thing was that I watched Christ manifest himself over and over again through my life. I was a dying man without Christ. *I could do nothing. And that was the key!*

I didn't understand it back then, but that was why I experienced the supernatural in my life. Whenever I had little faith in myself, God was able to move through me, even though I didn't fully realize why.

Every time God told me to do something, I disqualified my flesh as a candidate to accomplish the task and became absolutely desperate because I knew I couldn't do it in my own abilities. When God empowered me, gave me a word, or opened a door for me, it built my confidence and trust in Him.

On the other hand, because I didn't understand why the supernatural manifested some times but not others, I worked hard in my flesh toward becoming successful as a Christian. My deeds were good. But when I began to have physical problems, I didn't know what to do, because I didn't want to let others down. I compared myself to others who had gone through difficulties, and I fought to be as strong as I perceived them to be. I kept saying, "Be stronger, be successful, you're doing a good work for God."

The more I tried to impress God, the sicker and more depressed I became. Weeping on the steps of our ministry offices, I got low with Jesus. I kept saying, "Lord, I don't understand why I am so weak." The fact is *everyone is weak: If we weren't weak, we wouldn't need Jesus!* When we have Christ, we are strong, but it's His strength, not ours. When I pondered this, I had the first glimmer of understanding about dying to the flesh and allowing Christ to live though me. I was too tired anymore to play catch-up with the evangelical Joneses. I was sick of being proud, arrogant, and manipulative in my flesh. I had to get low with Jesus again.

When I did, He softly spoke to my heart, telling me to do the last thing I would ever have dreamed. He said to go to my father and confess my sins to him and have him pray for me. I could hardly believe it. Why tell my sins to a cruel man who abused me all my life? I didn't want to tell him I was deceitful, prideful, and sinful even though I was in ministry. What would he think? He had little enough respect for ministers as it was!

For years I had tried to lead my father to Christ. I preached, prodded, and poked literature at him. I tried to get him into every service I could. I fought for his attention, then came away defeated when he paid none. It had become a source of embarrassment to me that I could lead others to Christ but not my own father.

I was desperate, though, to get out of the depression I was in, so I tucked my tail between my legs, died to my flesh, and obeyed Christ. Every time I had done anything of any value for God, it was always following a state of total desperation, and this was no different.

I went to my father and said, "God told me to confess my sins to you and have you pray for me." I told him my long litany of sins, then I ducked my head as he laid his hands on me to pray. I had never wanted to feel those hands on me again. It was the hardest thing I could ever have done—humbling myself before that man, allowing him to touch me and even pray for me.

What I didn't know was that my father was eaten up with his own flesh. He was so full of his flesh that it was easy for him to repel me when I came at him in the same spirit—full of my flesh. But when I came to him in the opposite spirit, not exalting, accommodating, or feeding my flesh, he had nothing with which to resist the love of God. He prayed for me, and then He cried for the first time I had ever seen.

"I can never be saved because of what I did to you," he said with his head bowed.

"Yes, you can, Dad," I said. Right there, I led my father in the sinner's prayer and he was gloriously saved.

My father wasn't going to be saved by my religiosity and flesh preaching at him with all my doctrines. I had actually just been carrying out his heritage of fleshly living, merely on a different level of sanctification. Even though I was a minister, I was still walking after the flesh, just like him.

Humility is the badge of courage worn by all God-wrestlers.

CHAPTER NINE

The Great Omission

My zeal hath consumed me, because mine enemies have
forgotten thy words.
PSALM 119:139

The last mighty awakening, where the kingdom of God will rule and reign, is going to begin in the individual. It will be His lordship in my heart, Christ indwelling me, and my abiding in the Vine. From a practical standpoint, how do we get there?

Jesus looked upon Jerusalem and said, "Ye shall not see me henceforth, till ye shall say, 'Blessed is he that cometh in the name of the Lord'" (Matthew 23:39). "Ye" is you and me! We are blessed because we carry the name of the Lord. I believe Jesus was prophesying that there would be a people who would come in His name, filled with Him because they had been with Him, so the lost sheep would indeed see Jesus through them like a blinding light of glory.

They can't see He's blessed until they've been with Jesus in Spirit-to-spirit contact. Being with Jesus produces a manifestation of Jesus. When you've been with Him, revival fire is in your bones, and you have a warrior mentality to go beyond.

Men and women who have been with Jesus will be ruined for the natural. Their priorities change in an instant. They are freed from the power of this world system through the divine presence of Jesus alive in them. They become fully "pregnant" with the living Christ. The radiance of His glory in their lives triggers a heavenly response on a daily basis, turning ordinary people into fire-breathing, heaven-blessed, demon-scattering prophets of God.

Who Is This Christ in Us?

In the last decade we have embraced "who we are in Christ." Yet there is still the reality of *who Christ is in us*. During a recent conversation with Mike Atkins, a tremendous pastor and brother in the Lord who has been an enduring blessing to me personally, he named five stages of his own spiritual development, which I believe are likely experienced universally in the lives of believers:

1. *"God is against me."* We recognize our sinfulness in light of a holy God.

2. *"God is for me."* We learn that God is against our sin, but for us.

3. *"Christ is with me."* Christ becomes our companion, our friend.

4. *"Christ is in me."* Even though we generally ask Jesus to come inside during our prayer for salvation, we don't understand that He is actually, by His Spirit, living inside us (see Galatians 2:20).

5. *"I am in Christ in God."* The Bible constantly says Christ died for us and we're going to live for Him. Christ died in order to send His Spirit so that He could live through us.

At the third stage, "Christ is with me," we begin to depend upon Jesus. We find ourselves, throughout the day, praying, "Please help me, enable me, and give me the capacity to do this." This is where we've still only accepted Jesus as our assistant, so to speak. We're saying, "I'm going to do the preaching, the counseling, the evangelizing, the administrating, but I need your help."

Hudson Taylor, the first modern missionary to China, recorded his experience with this struggle in his journals. In his early days he prayed, *"Lord, give me the strength and power to do the work you've called me to do in China."* Two years into his mission, he stated, *"Lord, I pray you'll come alongside me and help."* A few years later he wrote, *"Lord, I pray that you will enable me to help you in the work that you're doing in China."* By the end of his life, he prayed, *"Lord, I pray you'll just get me out of your way so you can do your work, unhindered."*

The apostle Paul first said that he was "the least of the apostles" (1 Corinthians 15:9). Later he described himself as "less than the least of all saints" (Ephesians 3:8). Finally, near the end of his ministry, Paul called himself *the chief of all sinners* (see 1 Timothy 1:15).

> *Christ has made no provision for us to live our lives for Him. The only provision He made is for Him to live His life through us.*

We must move beyond trying to claim "maturity in Christ" because of the amount of Scripture we've learned or how long we've been members of "First Church." We must encourage each other to understand that Christ is in us, living His life through us, so therefore we are also in Christ. I've heard it said that Christ has made no provision for us to live our lives for Him. The only provision He made is for Him to live His life through us.

Christ is not just the Way and the Truth: He's also the Life (see John 14:6). He shows us the way and the truth, and then invites us along for an exciting ride—His living His life through ours.

It's Time We Break the Mold

Most Christians today seem to be stuck at the "Christ is with me" stage, having Christ as a companion. This is not wrestling with God. *This is a dating stage that lacks true intimacy.* Since we're frequently stuck in the same spot as most everyone around us, we think we have "arrived." This is where I was mired when Dr. Cho pointed out the next step: death to self. Eventually, some of us are going to have to break this cycle and lead our brothers and sisters out of spiritual immaturity.

Right now when one of us breaks the mold and starts doing the works of Christ, the rest of us clamor and pander as if we don't realize that the Holy Spirit living in that other person is the same Holy Spirit waiting for us in our own prayer closet. We need to move to the stage where Christ has residency and lordship because we have been with Him.

In 1988 the Middle East Peace Conference was about to begin at the Royal Palace in Madrid, Spain. The people were gathering; most of the Arab nations were to attend, along with representatives from the world's most powerful nations. Jesus whispered to me, *Go, Go, Go. There can be no peace conference without the Prince of Peace.*

I hastily flew to Madrid without hotel reservations. When I arrived, I asked the cab driver what was going on. He said Russian President Gorbachev and the Israeli Prime Minister Shamir were meeting for the first time at the Russian Embassy. Jesus prodded, *Go, be a witness unto me.* The hotel where all the ministers of the nations were staying was blocked to outsiders. I went there, and the Holy Spirit provided me a room. Then I had the cab take me quickly to the Russian Embassy.

It was raining, and freezing cold. We arrived at the gates of the embassy, and I jumped out and ran, clutching my *Thompson Chain Reference Bible.* When I found the correct gate, Russian camera crews were screaming to get in, but the man in charge was furious and would not let anyone enter. The anointing upon me felt strong, and I loudly said, "Who is in charge?" The man came over, and I said, "Open the gate and let me in."

He looked at me and asked for credentials. Instinctively, I lifted my Bible. He looked at it and turned his head in disgust to walk away. I said with a holy boldness, *"Come back, in Jesus' name!"*

When he spun around, I stuck my finger through the gate and said, *"Sir, in the name of the Lord Jesus Christ, who has sent me and whom I represent, open this gate and let me in."*

He pushed the button and pulled me through the gate as the Russian media bellowed. Tears streamed down my face as the glory of God filled me, bringing me as a witness for Him right into the Russian Embassy.

At the royal palace, door after door opened by the power of the Holy Spirit as I shared the Word of the Lord on six different occasions to the world press. To my knowledge, all of it was broadcast live in Israel.

One evening I talked with the Egyptian and Syrian foreign ministers. The Syrian asked if I was also a minister.

"Yes," I said.

"Of a country or kingdom?" he asked.

"Kingdom," I said.

"Oh, you are Semitic?" he asked.

"Yes I am Semitic."

"What kingdom?" he asked.

"Kingdom of God."

"I've never heard of that one. It must be very small."

"Oh no, it's the largest of all kingdoms. It would swallow up your kingdoms."

"You are very funny," they said, laughing.

I turned to the Egyptian foreign minister and said, "Sir, would you honor the esteemed words of your most famous prime minister and secretary of state who held two portfolios at the same time?"

"We never had such a man," he said.

"Yes, you did."

"If we did, I would have honored his words."

At that crucial peace conference, I picked up my Bible and read to one of the most powerful Egyptian ministers the story of Joseph, the Hebrew prime minister of Egypt who forgave his brothers! *Joseph was another God-wrestler.*

We must be dead to self but alive to Christ and ready for His present-day ministry to come alive within us and through us.

It's Never About Us, Always About Him

As I grew in Christ, I couldn't remember any role models or leaders explaining to me that I *couldn't* live the Christian life. So like anyone grateful to God for salvation, I tried to thrive on my own strength. I would brag, "I'll work the sixteen-hour days, because the work is worth it. I am driven by the burden I have for souls." It sounded so good and so right.

But while I received accolades from my peers for my efforts, my flesh became angry, bitter, irritable, cynical, and was physically breaking down under the load. *Anger, depression, lust, greed, and manipulation are all fruits of the self life.*

I didn't understand that I had missed the point entirely. My life revolved around ministry, not Christ. To me, the Christian life and "my" ministry were about self-effort. I interpreted every message I heard through the filter of what *I* needed to do rather than what *Christ* wanted to do in me if I would only relinquish control.

The Word says that *we enter into His rest when we cease from our own labors* (Hebrews 4:10). I am ashamed at how many years it took for me to do this.

Christ Is Alive Through the Holy Spirit

In the Old Testament, Jesus was alive here on earth by His Spirit. He showed himself to Moses, spoke to Daniel, and was seen by Isaiah. Abraham saw Jesus when he offered tithes to

Melchizedek. Jesus wrestled with Jacob. Before His birth on earth, Christ had manifested himself to others like Elijah, Noah, Enoch, and many more through Spirit-to-spirit contact. Prophets, priests, and kings were all transformed when they saw Jesus.

We read about those who were transformed in Old Testament days, when the anointing would "come and go" because there was no complete restoration between God and humankind without the finished work of Calvary. Now Christ has made a way for us to live in Him and He in us. We can't conquer the world. We've never been able to. We can't live the Christian life any more than the ancient Israelites could perfectly live according to the Mosaic Law. *But Christ can!*

For years I had Christ *with* me, and as I continued to pray and develop, I had Christ sometimes *in* my life, but I didn't have Christ *as* my life. In the Lord's Prayer, when Jesus said, "Thy kingdom come," He didn't mean He was setting up a kingdom where He would run for top office. He didn't need to be elected to anything, because He was already the King. He meant He was going to set up His kingdom *in us*. The present-day ministry of Jesus Christ operating in us is the fulfillment of His prayer, *"Thy kingdom come."*

Christ prayed, "Thy will be done on earth, as it is in heaven" (Matthew 6:10). God's will *is* the present-day ministry of Jesus Christ. It is done *in* us and *through* us, His children.

Jesus taught this prayer above everything else He could have taught the disciples in prayer because this is the most critical part of His mission. Then He went to heaven to send us the person of the Holy Spirit, through whom His present-day ministry would come.

Grafted Into the Vine of Christ

Christ is praying today that the kingdom will come within us. He is waiting for us to stop praying, "Lord, help me," as if He's doing something *to* us, and start recognizing that He is *in* us.

The apostle Paul said we were grafted into the covenant: *"Now you, too, receive the blessing God has promised Abraham and his children, sharing in God's rich nourishment of His own special olive tree"* (Romans 11:17 TLB). We were once like a wild olive branch and contrary to Christ. However, by virtue of our union with Him, we've broken off and been grafted into a cultivated olive branch, to share in Christ, the life-nourishing sap of the Vine.

We are no longer of Adam's vine. This means the life of Christ is not something added to our lives; *we're* added to *His.*

When you break off a branch (our old life), it's dead. When you graft it into the new Vine (Christ's life in us), it is resurrected. Once the branch is grafted, everything about the Vine becomes part of the branch. Our branch is now alive, but our Source of life is completely new. When we were grafted into Christ, we inherited the Vine's culture, history, and heritage. We're the same branch, but from now on we'll bear a different kind of fruit. The fruit we produce is the result of the life of its Source.

Some years ago Jesus softly told me to be a witness for Him to Yasser Arafat, the rabid anti-Semitic head of the Palestinian Liberation Organization (PLO). Arafat had been invited to a specially convened session of the United Nations in Geneva. I had no right to attend, but I flew to Geneva anyway and, through a blast of God's glory, ended up in the General Assembly, where I shared the gospel with dozens of diplomats.

One day Jesus instructed me to leave my briefcase in a certain room. I set it on a chair in the front, locked it, and left. To my amazement, Arafat announced a press conference that night, in that very room, with select PLO members and media. When I attempted to enter, I was stopped by security. I had no credentials, but I knew Jesus Christ had all the credentials in the world. I pointed out my briefcase, and they waved me through to my "reserved" seat—right across from Yasser Arafat! He made his speech and then said, "I shall allow three people to speak. Choose among yourselves."

The person of the Holy Spirit within me arose, and I boldly started preaching God's Word. "Shut up!" Arafat shouted. I continued, not knowing my words were being broadcast throughout the nation of Israel and the Middle East. When I finally stopped, Arafat and the PLO were so furious I believed someone in the room would try to kill me. Jesus whispered, *"Leave now, there will be a cab waiting with the door open. When you get back to your hotel, the phone will be ringing."* I saw an opening through the crowd and immediately exited out the back, speeding down the dark hallways. A cab was waiting at the side exit with its door open, and I safely stole away. *Wrestling with God means taking risks for His honor and glory.*

Arriving at my hotel room, the telephone was ringing; on the other end was the senior advisor to the Israeli prime minister, Dr. Reuben Hecht. He asked about my safety and whether or not I had bodyguards. I told him I had angels.

"Oh?" he said. "Good ones?"

"Yes, really good ones!" I said.

He asked me to speak to the nation of Israel the following day, after the speeches of the foreign minister and the ambassador. Again, God made me a bold witness as the present-day ministry of Jesus blasted through dead flesh.

Our goal is not to grit our teeth and try to produce fruit. We are called to abide in relationship with Him and not hinder the life-nourishing sap of the Vine from having full expression through our lives. Jesus expects us to bear the fruit that only He can produce.

In our instant inheritance of the Vine's history, everything Christ experienced, conquered, and achieved is ours. When we're saved, we're told we receive a new beginning and a new future. *But we don't often realize that we also receive a new past.*

When my branch was grafted into Christ, His history became legitimately mine. I can literally say Christ's stripes are my healer. His life is now my life. I'm not only legally but *organically* and *naturally* born again. I've been resurrected with Christ! I am literally in Christ, and therefore I'm a new creation. Old things have passed away, and all things have become new.

Our New Identity

For those of us who have struggled with our past, grafting into Christ is an absolutely amazing revelation. Everything that Jesus went through, *we've* gone through because we're in Him. We're part of His royalty, and His royalty is part of us. We no longer have to live in low self-esteem: We have the dignity of the life of Christ!

The healing, love, and acceptance we desire has been given to us perfectly in the person of Jesus. We are accepted in the Father. Our past, no matter how despicable, was totally and completely overcome when we were broken off the old branch and grafted into the new Vine.

I used to excuse myself from dying to the flesh because *I* needed to control the repairs on myself: fixing rejections, hurts, wounds, inadequacies, insecurities, and fears is a never-ending cycle. We can't be about God's business if we invest our energies into fixing our flesh. We don't need to, and we can't. We were grafted into Christ so at last we could have a good past.

Trying to see the future from the perspective of our past causes us to see it through our fears and failures. And dragging our past failures into our present hinders us from embracing God's dream for our future. *When we hold on to what's happened, we drag our failures into what's coming.*

It's a worthless endeavor to spend the rest of our lives trying to sanctify our flesh as a form of apology to Jesus for our past. Satan is only successful in holding things over our heads if we embrace our past as though it is who we are. It's a lie. *Our past is swallowed up in the Resurrection!*

I recently talked with someone who was bound by the shame of certain mistakes he had made. It hit me that *the more we rehearse our past and repeatedly apologize for it, the more we re-curse it because we regret it. And the more we re-curse it, the harder it is to reverse it.* The apostle Paul had a terrible past to overcome; he must have sat in church with the widows of the men he'd put to death before his conversion. Think of the guilt! But when Paul embraced Christ's past, it became His past. Rehearsing it or re-cursing it makes it impossible to reverse it.

Saul's identity before he became Paul was in *what he did* (see Galatians 1:13–14). Paul's identity after his experience on the road to Damascus was in *who he was in Christ*. When our identity is in what we do, we will constantly feel unworthy, because our works fail. This identity trap keeps us in a cycle of deception, working harder and harder to get approval, while Jesus weeps because we nullify His blood (see 1 Corinthians 1:17).

Most people have a hero. We tend to copy that person. We tend to talk like our favorite Christians, preach like them, study like them, and read the same Bible translation. Instead of being with Jesus, we reach out to a person we can emulate. This is a subtle seduction to move away from God through a sincere desire to draw close to Him. With the best of intentions, we surrender the royal scepter.

We become disillusioned with our heroes because we identify with their flesh. In middle age, Christian men and women get divorced because their identity is in their flesh. The mom, when the kids are grown, can't find her identity apart from them. The dad, replaced as a manager by a younger man, is crushed because his identity is in his job.

When our foundation of trust is built upon the imperfect and insufficient works of our flesh, we become fear-filled control freaks. Our identity as preachers should not be in preaching but in Jesus. Our identity as believers is not in our jobs, kids, grades, or bank accounts. It's in Jesus. When we identify ourselves with Jesus, we open the door for His present-day ministry to begin.

My wife, Carolyn, and I were once inadvertently assigned to separate rows on a short flight. Seated behind her, I started to share the gospel with the man next to me. Suddenly the woman next to Carolyn started crying. When my wife inquired the reason, she said she wished the man preaching could help her. "That's my husband!" Carolyn exclaimed.

We traded seats, and I discovered the woman, whose name was Lucy, had come from England in a last hope to cure inoperable malignant tumors. I prayed for her, but didn't sense the Spirit moving. Six weeks later, though, Lucy wrote to us from England, saying that after rigorous examinations in the U.S. and at home, neither doctor could find a trace of cancer! Hallelujah!

We can't fix our lives, change ourselves, or become on our own what God wants us to be. God can change us if we realize that heaven does not revolve around us but around Christ. *We can only become God-wrestlers.*

Our Testimony Is Christ's Testimony

The desire for a magnificent destiny, and a life of meaning and purpose, was given to us because Jesus promised we could rule and reign with Him forever. We don't only have a wonderful future, we also have a wonderful past with Him. We must accept Christ's past in order to accept His future.

The Bible says believers overcome "by the blood of the Lamb and by the word of their testimony" (Revelation 12:11). What this implies is that we are victorious through *His* testimony: "Our people defeated Satan because of the blood of the Lamb and *the message of God*" (CEV, emphasis added). We don't overcome the evil one by telling him about how bad we were when we took drugs. We overcome the evil one by telling him that we are in Christ.

Your testimony isn't your life story; your testimony is Christ's witness in you. The testimony by which we overcome is the relinquishing of control, and by Jesus reigning within us. Our testimony is that we were crucified with Christ and yet we live. *Our testimony is His testimony.*

A king cannot rule unless he understands he is the heir to the throne. He comprehends his destiny by belief in the fullness of his bloodline. Jesus said we are kings and queens. Our dignity and our destiny are in Christ.

Your testimony isn't your life story; your testimony is Christ's witness in you.

The enemy has tried to pervert our identity, to compel us to glorify what we were instead of Christ's finished work. But the Bible says,

Fear ye not, neither be afraid: have not I told thee from that time, and have declared it? Ye are even my witnesses. Is there a God beside me? Yea, there is no God; I know not any. (Isaiah 44:8)

When all we do is look back, it seems we've come a long way, so we settle down instead of pressing along on our journey of faith.

Jesus already overcame Satan when He was tempted on the mount (Luke 4:5–6) by speaking the Word of God, and we overcome the adversary the same way. Instead of resisting Satan with a hopeful prayer, we resist him in full confidence, standing on the Word of God (through which he was already defeated) and speaking it out.

I was praying one morning in a Jacksonville hotel, and Jesus whispered, *Go eat breakfast now.* I went. It was early, and there was only one man in the restaurant. Jesus urged, *Go have breakfast with him.* I didn't know the man, but I sat down and said, "Good morning, how are you? What are you having for breakfast?"

He told me, and I said, "Me too."

I asked how his family was. He thought surely he must know me because I was sitting with him, but he couldn't remember from where. Finally, embarrassed, he said, "I'm so sorry. I've forgotten who you are."

"That's because you've never met me."

"What! I've never met you?"

"That's right."

"Then why are you having breakfast with me?"

"I've been sent here."

"By whom?"

"I'm a hit man."

"A what?"

"A hit man—a Holy Spirit hit man. There's a contract out on you." I lifted my Bible and set it on the table. "I've been sent by Jesus Christ."

He started laughing. "I have nine generations of Greek Orthodox preachers in my genealogy," he said.

I smiled. "That's not an American Express card to heaven. You can believe in your head, but until Christ comes into your heart, you're a lost man."

I discovered he was discouraged, and I was able to share the gospel of Jesus Christ with him. Then he allowed me to pray with him. He was an ABC sports commentator known as "Jimmy the Greek."

If we're drawn into Jesus, because Jesus is drawn into us, there comes a point of contact where the past becomes the present and the present becomes the past. *We live in the now with Christ.*

Steps to Achieve Our Destiny

Our problem is not how to make Christ work within us more effectively; our problem is how to get ourselves *in Christ.*

We've recognized that self has been on the throne in our lives. We've admitted what we're not. We've stopped pretending we're better than we are, praying as if we can fool God into believing our words instead of looking at our hearts. We've opened our-selves so Jesus can fuse who He is with what we aren't. We've acknowledged our desire to fulfill His destiny for us, to be part of the latter-rain outpouring of God's Spirit.

We've crucified our flesh, made no provision for it, and deter-mined not to entertain it. We've rid ourselves of every hindrance:

ego, pride, and idolatry. We've laid down vulgarity and our love of the world at Christ's feet.

Now we have to obey. Instantly. Totally. We would annul our own prayers if we walked away from the altar, out of the prayer closet, and returned to the same disobedience we practiced the day before, last year, or a decade ago. Author Ed Cole says,

An ounce of obedience is worth a pound of prayer.

Everything Christ did was for a purpose. He knew no wasted moments or wasted days. He has already planned the mission and the ministry; our part is to obey.

Throughout Scripture, we see that men like Gideon, Moses, and Abraham went forward obediently, and *then* they were empowered. Human obedience directly correlates with heavenly authorization, as God-wrestlers well know.

The Father wants to release and authorize the power. He doesn't want us flying around in a holding pattern any more than we do. Through our obedience we become like Jesus with a passion to please the Father.

Once in the 1980s Dr. Cho asked me to preach for him. Since my early days in the military, I had prayed each day on the mountain that Dr. Cho later bought and named Prayer Mountain. I have always felt close to his church. I was eagerly anticipating the honor of ministering there as I checked into my hotel room in Seoul to seek the Lord for His direction on the message.

When I prayed, Jesus softly said, *"Go to Dr. Cho and tell him you cannot preach for him."*

God knew I wanted to preach there so I could tell everyone that I had preached at the largest church in the world. When the Lord challenged me, I struggled with Him, but finally agreed to obey. I repented before Dr. Cho, admitting my pride and my desire to preach only because of the large size of his church and not for the souls that would be saved. I left Korea embarrassed.

My next meeting was in Pennsylvania at a "Jesus Fest" in a

muddy field outside of Hershey. I'll never forget looking around at that squalid venue and thinking, *I could have been at the largest church in the world instead of sloshing around out there.* A man asked me to go with him to pray for a woman in a trailer. She was dying from at least sixteen incurable diseases and living in a room covered with plastic. Her body was huge with fluid retention, and her skin was scaly. I prayed a simple prayer, sensed nothing, and left.

A year later I went back to that area, and a woman greeted me, reminding me of the incident. I thought she was perhaps the sick woman's daughter, but instead she said, "That was me."

Jesus gently spoke to my heart: *Son, this is what happens when you're willing to be obedient. This is what happens when you seek my favor instead of man's.*

I learned a valuable lesson.

There is a dynamic that transcends the natural mind, natural responses, and normal Christianity; it attracts the glory of God, the purposes of God, and the destiny of God. *We must obey in order to see that dynamic operate in our lives.*

CHAPTER TEN

Jesus on the Throne

And I beheld, and, lo, in the midst of the throne and
of the four beasts, and in the midst of the elders,
stood a Lamb as it had been slain.
REVELATION 5:6

Once we've been with Jesus, we'll never be content living our lives without a passion for God's glory and for personal purity. *Spiritual passion is a hallmark of one who wrestles with God.* When we're *not* with Jesus, we become territorial; willing to attack any "prey" that crosses the boundaries of our flesh; filled with the ability to disgrace the reputation of the King of Glory; indifferent to polluting the holiness of the purpose of God in our lives.

Barrenness Testifies Against Us

We can become so bound by our flesh that we can sit through a Spirit-led service and never feel conviction. We can speak the name of Christ and at the same time, unknowingly, be declaring war against the Cross by our lives. We can fellowship with the saints while being totally unrepentant. *In this state, all we manifest is fruitlessness.*

We are barren in reaching souls for Christ because barrenness is the fruit of not being with Jesus. We fight to allow self to maintain its right to the throne, and our barrenness testifies against us. Christ's divine mission does not revolve around us. *He* is the King of Glory. Many of us act as if the Holy Spirit was sent as a spiritual bellhop to run errands for us!

In our instant-everything society, we become discouraged when the promised fruit doesn't immediately bloom on the tree. Impatience separates the goats from the true sheep that willingly follow their Master at any price.

On one occasion in prayer, I pictured a toe, a thumb, and an ear inside a womb. The womb is Christ within us, yet entire Christian sects are established when someone sees just His thumb and worships it. Another sees God's ear and starts a movement where people copy each other, everyone acting like ears. Or we rejoice over a toe and organize First Toe Assembly. People are excited they have seen the toe and, hallelujah, are part of the toe! We think we're pregnant with Christ, filled with His glory, when the only thing coming out of the womb is His foot!

Christ does not want to reveal His thumb, His ear, or His toe: Christ wants to reveal His face. When we behold Him, there is no boasting and no religious pride—just brokenness, reverence, and the glory of God. Without seeing His face, we take tremendous pride in the part of God we think we've captured: "I have the Holy Spirit" or "I'm an evangelist." God wants us to seek His face, being dissatisfied with merely being part of Thumb Fellowship or the Ear Connection. *God wants us to have all of Him, just as He is to have all of us.*

We have been content to live our Christian life in a comfort zone, a state that cost us nothing. It's a cheap, tidy form of

Christianity, void of sacrifice and "embarrassment." We don't get dirty when we don't get low.

The only power that will transform this world is the power of Jesus, flowing through a person who has been with Him. The devil understands one thing—a man or woman of God with a bigger stick than his. That bigger stick is Jesus.

> The Spirit is crying, "Wake up, mighty men, wake up, mighty women! I'm going to visit my bride with a heavenly power surge!"

Resurrection power in the lives of believers will ignite an unparalleled fire. Many of us are D.O.A. (Dead On Arrival), hardhearted, content with dead religion, instead of being armed and dangerous. Satan will sing right along with us as long as we keep increasing and Christ keeps decreasing. He will happily keep the rest of the world in bondage while he's blinding us to Christ's face. A hunger is growing in God's people—a desire to do what they have signed up to do. *We want to be filled, to be with Jesus, and we will pay any price. We are God-wrestlers.*

One day I was praying in a hotel room, when I had a vision of a man outside weeping with his face to the ground, leaning his head on a ball. Jesus softly said, *"Go to the restaurant. You are to be a witness to that man."*

When I went to the restaurant, a man who had played for the Boston Celtics rushed over to say, "Man, I love you! When you shared the gospel at a pre-game chapel, I was saved. Then God saved my marriage, my career, and my life. I've always wanted to thank you. God bless you."

I smiled, thanking God for sending me downstairs, thinking that was that. Then the restaurant filled with some of the most famous basketball players in America. When I finished my breakfast, Jesus said, *"Pay their bill."*

"Lord, they're millionaire basketball players!"

"Pay their bill." There must have been over twenty players in

that room, and I'd watched them—they ate big!

"Pay their bill." So I did.

That afternoon one of the players sent someone over to thank me, inviting me to dinner to return the favor. Over dinner, I shared the gospel with him. It was Michael Jordan. In prayer, I had seen him crying after winning the NBA championship (following the death of his father). I was able to tell him about God the Father weeping for the death of Jesus, His Son.

Lord, deliver us from being full of ourselves, being easily offended, living with a competitive spirit, nursing unbridled anger, bragging about our self-worth—consumed by self-pity, self-consciousness, and selfishness—as the world hungrily awaits a touch from you.

Dry Bones Are an Army Waiting to Happen!

The Cross is a revelation to humankind that all works of the flesh are completely void of merit with God. No matter how religious or sincere, no human righteousness can contribute to the glorious person of Jesus Christ. When we subscribe to natural solutions to our struggles, we neutralize the power of the Atonement.

The flesh desires to conquer the Cross and to compete for His blood. *The Cross desires to conquer the flesh and eradicate its lordship!* By nature, we want to follow Jesus from the manger to the mansion, bypassing the cross.

> **By nature, we want to follow Jesus from the manger to the mansion, bypassing the cross.**

The prophet Ezekiel had a vision of the dry, bleached bones of utterly lifeless corpses. *This is our flesh.* Dead, powerless ministers preach dead sermons to dead, powerless congregations—and everyone wonders why a lost and dying world cannot see Jesus.

> Again he said unto me, "Prophesy upon these bones, and say unto them, 'O ye dry bones, hear the word of the

LORD. . . . I will cause breath to enter into you, and ye shall live: And I will . . . cover you with skin, and put breath in you, and ye shall live; and ye shall know that I am the LORD.'" So I prophesied as I was commanded. (Ezekiel 37:4–7)

Ezekiel saw a mighty shaking of dead bones. That's precisely what we need, but it cannot be gained through religion that does not exalt Christ above all. When Ezekiel's bones stood upon their feet, they were an exceedingly great army. God is raising up a mighty army, alive and filled with His glory. *The Holy Spirit causes dry bones to live.*

In America alone, fifty-seven million people profess Christ as Lord. However, because of the carnality of our lives, the lost pursue other gods and idols; the army of God spends most of its time "keeping people saved" and helping backsliders slide back to God. Thousands and thousands of denominations worldwide were created by church splits, with millions of intramural micro splits. The prophets during Ahab and Jezebel's wicked reign spent their time comforting or competing with each other instead of confronting demons. Millions come to our Christ-ian "sales meetings" only to discard the product when they go home. *The world is not impressed with people who claim Jesus but don't God-wrestle.*

Religion is a sorry substitute for the pure presence of Christ. Religion rewards those who claw their way to the top, pushing aside the sweet Savior, substituting their religious nature for His righteousness. Those who idolize religion know nothing of surrender; it's about fighting for *their* rights instead of fighting for *His* honor. Not everyone will aspire to be a God-wrestler, but for those of us who do, we say, *Be gone, unrepentant, uncrucified flesh—flesh filled with self-righteousness, self-admiration, self-sufficiency, self-love, and self-confidence! Give us Christ!*

For years the Pensacola revival was carried on every major news outlet. What will the world think when they see Christ's present-day ministry as a mighty, triumphant army of God with

His true mission as their battle cry?

Let the Cross do its deadly work to slay our flesh so that Resurrection power can change and empower us to reach a lost and dying world.

The kingdom of God has come! We can no longer settle for knowing *about* Him. Because we're convinced that *we* need to accomplish what *only* Christ can do, the flesh tries to control our churches instead of allowing Christ at the helm. The enemy has desensitized us and clouded our understanding of our priestly role, which can only be entered into when we fully comprehend the greatness of what Christ has accomplished.

We must rise up as Paul did, daily emptying the flesh in the same way we take out the trash. As an act of his will, through the power of the Holy Spirit, Paul did not give the flesh the right to lord over Him. He also refused to backslide: He died to his own desires, ambitions, reputation, and purposes, allowing Christ to rule and reign through him. He made the main thing *the main thing:* Christ in him, the hope of glory.

Following Paul's example allows the Spirit to circumcise our heart until God's glory roars through us, revealing the face of Christ. Paul was circumcised in his heart, and all those who wrestle with God will need to be: "If ye live after the flesh, ye shall die: but if ye through the Spirit do mortify the deeds of the body, ye shall live" (Romans 8:13).

Paul put no confidence in the flesh but counted everything as loss for the knowledge of *Him.* How often have we settled for applauding God's people because they preach well or sing beautifully? We've reduced the present-day ministry of Jesus Christ to a spectator sport, cheering for our spiritual heroes. If we don't know Christ, we can't live in Him.

Open our eyes that we might see, O God, and deliver us from religious smugness and contentment. Do not allow sin to blur our vision of Jesus. Lord, let your Son shine like the sun through us, manifested through the person of the Holy Spirit. May we be mirrors that reflect your glory. This is the hour of your unimaginable visitation. Direct us toward Mount Zion, the City of the Living God, the heavenly Jerusalem, and an innumerable company of angels, to the General Assembly, and the Church of the Firstborn.

Being With Jesus, Day by Day

My flesh can *rot* in the status quo, but it cannot *die* without something to replace it; what is needed is the life of Christ. We can only embrace the Christ of the present by embracing the Christ of the past, the Christ who made himself of no reputation on our behalf; the Christ who learned obedience by the things He suffered; the Christ who lived to do the will of the Father; the Christ who completely died to His flesh and was crucified; the Christ who was gloriously resurrected.

We'll never be with Jesus in His present, supernatural power unless we embrace His Cross. Many Christians shun it, calling it "legalism," but still rejoice in the revelation that we are more than conquerors in Christ Jesus. *How* are we going to become more than conquerors? Can we conquer without the Cross? No chance. We must die to the flesh, accept the ministry of Christ, and move into Spirit-to-spirit contact.

Being with Jesus is not about *playing* the part of a Christian soldier—it's about *being* the part. Being with Christ cannot be reduced to a quick session where we pick up the Bible, write in a journal, pray, and then leave. We must become consciously aware that in every second of our lives, with every breath we take, and with every beat of our hearts, we are part of Christ.

I can't imagine sitting down with my wife, Carolyn, and saying, "I'll spend fifteen minutes with you in the morning. I'll contemplate and adore you, then I'll confess any bad feelings or attitudes I've had toward you. I'll take another five minutes to praise you. After that, I'll tell you what I need you to do for me, and I'll only have time again for you the following morning." *That would create tension, not intimacy.*

The present-day ministry of Jesus Christ will not fully function until we have been with Him. Praying selfishly and repetitively accomplishes little; praying as if our life depended on it accomplishes much, because, in fact, it does. Being with Christ is not a matter of minutes or hours in a day. Being with Christ is a fusion, where we're seated together with Jesus in heavenly places in a constant state of fellowship with God.

We must not close our Bibles and walk away from our quiet time with a smug feeling that we're "done," crossing it off our list for the day. We miss the most important part of our relationship with Christ when we click off and go in our own direction. *If we reduce being with Jesus to a small part of each day, we miss the works and words He is yearning to express through us* all *day.* Jesus said He did what He saw the Father doing. The words He spoke were not His but the words the Father gave Him to speak. *Christ is our example.*

He wants us to abide in Him, and He in us, every minute of every day, consciously aware of who He is and what He is doing within us. Once we've been with Jesus, nothing else matters. All that matters is the living, breathing, abiding Spirit within us, manifesting Christ's ministry through us to complete His mission.

Will We Birth Jesus?

We are not human beings having a spiritual experience; *we are spiritual beings having a human experience.* Christ said He left this earth so His Spirit could reside within us. The fulfillment of His purposes in our lives carries a price. It may cause discomfort, inconvenience, and even pain. This is what it cost a young Jewish woman named Miriam, whom we commonly refer to as Mary, the mother of Jesus.

Two thousand years ago Jesus manifested himself in the womb of Mary, who was likely a teenager. Mary became full of God's life by the Holy Spirit (Matthew 1:18–20). She was entrusted with the greatest responsibility on earth—to bear the Son of the living God and bring a Savior into the world. God entrusted to Mary His own seed, His own Son, so she would carry, birth, nurture, and raise Him.

Today, Jesus wants a body to possess with all His power.

Mary would never have aborted Jesus, although it would have been socially expedient because of the pressure and humiliation placed upon her and Joseph. She would never have exploited Jesus; she would never have given Him up because of the severe inconvenience to her young marriage; she would never have hindered His ministry when His first teachings embarrassed the family. Instead, she yielded, enduring all of the discomfort and inconvenience, and brought forth a Savior into the world. Keeping within her heart the things He said, she released Him to fulfill His destiny.

Today, Jesus Christ still delegates to the weakest believer the rights to His name, the keys to His kingdom, authority over the earth, and all power to represent Him. That person can refuse Jesus because He isn't politically correct. That person can abuse Christ's power in order to endorse and enlarge his own flesh. That person can obfuscate Christ's reputation and exploit His name. That person can also choose not to do one thing with what Jesus gave him.

The final visitation is not about a woman giving birth to the Son of God; it's about ordinary people allowing the person of the Holy Spirit to penetrate the self life so fully and completely that no longer will the world see anything but the present-day ministry of Jesus Christ.

Rather than being an echo of a man-pleasing, flesh-fed generation who has self on the throne of our lives, the Son of Righteousness shall rise with healing in His wings, setting hungry and thirsty believers ablaze, starting the greatest outpouring of the Holy Spirit the world has ever known and thrusting God-wrestlers beyond anything they could ever imagine—into a realm of glory where they will be seated together with Jesus in heavenly places and filled with the measure of the stature of the fullness of

Christ. They will know they are people of destiny, the final generation that will gather the final harvest, ushering in the Lord's return. They will not simply go through the Word but will allow the Word to go through them. *We have a divine appointment with destiny.*

Trying to control how much of His life will come through ours, we say, in essence, "Jesus, I only want you on *my* terms," which is tantamount to rebellion. Yet we say we're "filled" with the Holy Spirit, not even understanding that the primary mission of the Spirit is to manifest the life of Christ through us. When we hinder the manifestation of Jesus, we challenge God over throne rights and grieve His Spirit.

When we are intimate with Christ, we become pregnant with God's visions: Our spirits must become impregnated with the dreams, visions, passions, ambitions, and strategies of the King of Glory. He must become alive and fully functional within us. Men of God have achieved this oneness. The anointing upon Enoch was so powerful that he was taken up into glory by the Spirit of Christ (Hebrews 11:5). *He literally wrestled his way into Christ's presence!* Christ has again come in Spirit, but in even greater measure because of the finished work of the Cross. Spirit-to-spirit contact is no longer God anointing us—it is the Father anointing Jesus Christ who is within us.

Just as a woman who is pregnant, when we are full of Christ's mission, we become overwhelmed by that which is within us in everything we do. We're consumed with the nurturing process every waking moment. It interrupts our sleep, our dreams, and our visions. It's part of our bloodstream and like the air we breathe. Everything we have is invested in it. It becomes who we are. *Spirit-to-spirit contact consumes us because we're full of the revelation of the present-day ministry of Jesus Christ.* We say, like Mary, "Behold, the handmaid of the Lord [I am Your servant]; be it unto me according to thy word" (see Luke 1:38). Our heart's cry is *"Whatever He says, do it!"*

We're carrying Jesus, and Jesus is carrying us. Christ is in us, and we are in Christ. We're no longer struggling with the load of the Christian life. As the unborn child is sustained by its mother's body, so we feast on the fullness of the Father. We share the same blood, the same metabolism, the same breath, and the same life. When we enter this fusion of Spirit-to-spirit contact, Christ is released in us with all His glory and power.

Men, women, boys, and girls should become unable to separate themselves from Christ. As we are pregnant with Christ's ministry, in the fullness of time, we are empowered for the assignment that no demon in hell, no kingdom on earth, and no principality in the universe will be able to stop: releasing the strategic manifestation of the glory of Jesus. With the present-day ministry of Christ, the Bible's provocative proclamations—such as "a glorious church without spot or wrinkle" and "a perfect man, unto the measure of the stature of the fullness of God"—will come into the brightness of the Lord's glory.

Jesus did what the Father did because Jesus died completely to His own flesh: "Though He were a Son, yet learned He obedience by the things which He suffered" (Hebrews 5:8). Christ was willing to sacrifice His dreams, His visions, everything He had for His bride. *When we empty ourselves, willing to obey for the sake of Christ, instead of fighting for our rights, we allow the present-day ministry of Jesus to be manifested through us in all of His glory.*

Not Religion or Tradition

The apostle John was imprisoned on Patmos, an Aegean island off the southwestern coast of Asia Minor (see Revelation 1:9). Surrounded by depraved human beings, he was still able to enter into intimate relationship with Christ and see the Lord. Even though he had walked physically with Jesus on earth, he was radically transformed as he beheld the revelation of the glorified Savior. What the world needs is not religion or tradition. *We need to see Jesus walking right off the pages of the gospel, the living reality of the resurrected Lord.*

Intimacy with Christ cannot be achieved in groups. Alone with Christ, we fall in love with Him.

For at least two decades, church leaders have tried to achieve unity with ecumenical movements, but the greatest unifier is the power of God. Christ doesn't attend one church: His body *is* the church. The prayer of agreement, simply agreeing for this great outpouring of God, will bring us into unity as a true body of believers. God's mind and power will be released to us as we fall in love with Jesus, full of His mission and coming together in agreement.

Jesus said, "I and my Father are one" (John 10:30) and "He that hath seen me hath seen the Father" (John 14:9). Christ's life gives us a revelation of the empowerment engendered when a believer comes into agreement with the Father. Such agreement absolutely transforms the world. God is going to raise up an army of believers who have been with Jesus and who will leave a ministry trail of freed and healed people wherever they go. *God is going to release, on the earth, the God-wrestlers.*

Agreement in prayer results in the *commanded* blessing of God. "Agreement" in Hebrew is the word *echod;* the words *shomé à Israeli adoni shelkha eloha echod* mean "Hear, O Israel, the Lord thy God, the Lord is One." This is the first prayer every Jew learns. Passionate intercession is like the anointing that came down the head of Aaron to the hem of his garment. Every Old Testament Jew who changed the world received the commanded blessing through agreement with God.

Everyone who has been with Christ receives God's commanded blessing. God is waiting. The angels are waiting. The kingdom is waiting. All heaven is waiting for you to be with Jesus and release Him in all His fullness and glory, to fulfill His destiny and not hinder Him.

Mary did not grieve the person of the Holy Spirit. She committed herself to cooperate with the plan of God to manifest the Savior. Like Mary, we know precisely who is in our "womb." Our most important mission is to be with Jesus and allow His face to be revealed through us to a lost and dying world.

Old Testament law reads,

If men strive, and hurt a woman with child, so that her fruit depart from her, and yet no mischief follow: he shall be surely punished, according as the woman's husband will lay upon him; and he shall pay as the judges determine. (Exodus 21:22)

The striving, fleshly spirit is a spirit of abortion and murder. When we operate in the flesh, we're kicking at the womb of the Holy Spirit. The Father wants us to birth Spirit-to-spirit contact, but He cannot achieve this in the life of a believer who is consumed with selfish ambition and vain conceit.

Our Blessed Hope

When we first become Christians, we have high expectations of what was promised, but we receive little.

Hope deferred makes the heart sick, but a desire fulfilled is a tree of life. (Proverbs 13:12 NRSV)

We become disillusioned that the victorious Christian life is just "preacher talk" because we don't understand the dynamic of being in Christ. We cannot become more than conquerors if we have not learned that our lives must be hid in Him.

In the biblical account of Hannah, her womb was closed, causing a broken and wounded spirit. In that time women received their self-image from children, and Hannah was barren, feeling like a failure in her performance as a wife. In her brokenness, Hannah couldn't distinguish the voice of the Lord from the voice of defeat. But she became immune to irritation as she poured out her heart in the house of the Lord. She was a woman who knew how to wrestle with God, and as she "prayed through," she made a promise:

If thou wilt look on the affliction of thine handmaid, and remember me, and . . . give unto thine handmaid a man child, then I will give him unto the LORD all the days of his life. (1 Samuel 1:11)

At the temple, the priest noticed Hannah and said her prayer would be answered. Later she returned with her son, Samuel, and declared, "Mine horn is exalted in the LORD" (1 Samuel 2:1). Hannah received a changed self-image when she delivered her child. In the same way, we cannot fix ourselves, but we can carry Jesus and birth His ministry in this decaying world.

Will we refuse Jesus while we concentrate on fixing our poor self-image? Will we refuse Jesus because we're too embarrassed to carry Him? Or will we bear Jesus, understanding the Holy Word that is in our womb?

The Spirit within us is the same Spirit within Jesus, who walked through the Old Testament and visited prophets, priests, and kings, only more glorious now because of His redemptive blood. *Will we let His anointing flow in our lives?*

CHAPTER ELEVEN

Look on Us

He [Jesus] was wounded for our transgressions, he was bruised for
our iniquities. . . . And with his stripes we are healed.
ISAIAH 53:5

If the greatest power on earth, the Spirit of Christ, dwells in you,
He will enliven and revitalize you (see Romans 8:11). The Spirit-
to-spirit power surge quickens and transforms, releasing in us a
manifestation of Christ that causes others to know we have been
with Jesus. If we haven't been with Him, the power shuts down;
the lights may flicker, but there's nobody home. Once again, God
cannot empower exalted flesh, even if self is exalting itself through
religiosity or sincerity.

The only earth-shaking possession of the early church was the
knowledge that they had been with Jesus. They knew who was
within them, giving them power to revolutionize the world. The
coming great awakening is about the indwelling King of Glory

kicking down the gates of hell. Christ in you is the only hope to transform a lost and dying world.

To become part of the final awakening and qualify for Christ's power, the Father must verify that we have been with Jesus. That's all. Jesus said,

> "Listen! I am standing at the door, knocking; if you hear my voice and open the door, I will come in to you and eat with you, and you with me" (Revelation 3:20 NRSV).

Jesus wants to be with us more than we want to be with Him! And He will, if we'll die to self and open the door for Him through wrestling in prayer. He won't open it from His side; we must open it from ours.

Jesus is intent on being Jesus in us. As we enter, through prayer, into intimacy with Him, God will plunge us into a river of change, transforming us into the image of Christ so the world will know we have been with Jesus. We will no longer need to advertise our affiliation or brag about our religious "dog tags." The person of the Holy Spirit will fill us, like He did Peter, until even our shadows are filled with the glory of God. Then we will know the eternal weight of the phrase *Jesus Christ is Lord*. Our focus will no longer be on what we've done but on who Christ is now.

God is putting His finger on critical issues, provoking us to evaluate our direction and commitment, becoming willing to change. Revival fires are burning. God is seeking out men and women who will cry, *"Here am I; send me!"* (see Isaiah 6:8). These are the God-wrestlers.

With flesh on the throne of our lives, we are lowered from God's divine purpose into a dimension where we can't understand His will. Christ's first command in the gospel of Mark is "Repent!" In the Greek (from *metanoia*), this means "Change your mind!" Repentance is an ongoing spiritual revolution that doesn't end with justification. God's magnificent gift of eternal life is the *entrance* into a river of change, turning ingrained attitudes inside out. Jesus said we are to take up our cross, lose our life, and follow Him (see Matthew 16:24–25). When we return to the Cross, Jesus is lifted up and draws people to God (see John 12:32). We cannot afford to live a Christianity that costs us nothing; Christ's sacrifice cost Him everything.

The flesh desires to conquer and disregard the lordship of the Cross. The Cross would overcome the flesh and eradicate its lordship. The revelation of Christ fulfilling His destiny in the now is contingent upon our embracing the Cross and committing ourselves to the purposes for which Jesus laid down His life. *That's* when we qualify for the earthly mission of Christ. It's more than singing about the wondrous cross on which the Prince of Glory died. *It's offering our bodies as living sacrifices.*

The coming awakening will only be triggered by prayer— agonized repentance, deep intercession, and God-wrestling obedience—until we know we've been with Jesus. This will enable Him to finish His work on earth through us, becoming the final heavenly spark that ignites the greatest awakening in world history and ushers in the return of Christ. Only by repenting and seeking God will we experience the delegated ministry of Jesus.

Father, open our eyes so that we realize we have spent much time sitting in our religious bleachers, idolizing stars rather than allowing the Holy Spirit to burn unsanctified flesh out of our lives so that the world can behold the Bright and Morning Star.

The World Will See Jesus

Once when I was in prayer Jesus softly told me: *"I will open up Russia to you."* Years ago I had purchased and restored the home of Corrie ten Boom because of my tremendous love for what she did to rescue the Jewish people. Jesus instructed me to go to that home in Haarlem, Holland. I did, and as I prayed there, a woman came and invited me to have dinner with her and her husband. *I had never met her before, yet Jesus said that her husband would be the key to Russia.*

Sitting in their home that evening, I began to weep uncontrollably. When they asked why, I told the husband that the Holy Spirit had told me that God had put His hand on him, and that he would be used as a major key in proclaiming the gospel in Russia. Shocked, he told me he owned more than one hundred corporations in Russia, was a personal friend of the president, and had just led the head of the KGB to Christ. He served as a door to reach many for Christ.

Some time later, as I was privately worshiping the Lord, Jesus whispered, *"You will preach the gospel in the Kremlin."* I flew to Moscow and asked the officials if I could speak. They said no. I went back again, and they said no. Seventeen times they said no. But I knew what God had said. When I asked for the eighteenth time, they said yes. Among the words in my message at the Kremlin Palace were *"Stalin is dead, Lenin is dead, but Jesus Christ is alive."*

More than seventy-two hundred Russians came to Christ that night, and we gave New Testaments to all of them. Our message was televised to the entire national audience of more than one hundred million people, the first such Russian broadcast with an altar call. People had said it was impossible. *What is impossible with man is possible with God. The world will see Jesus!*

One four-star Russian general was so angry he threatened, *"I ought to kill you now, and bury you under the concrete of the Kremlin Palace for what you have said."* I looked into his eyes, and as I did, the tears started flowing down my face: *"I love you, [and] Jesus loves you."* When I reached my arms around him, I could hear him sobbing. I knew what was going on. What a joy it was to pray with him as he received Jesus as his Lord and Savior.

Satan was possessed with his own ambition and his own pride, the seed of which went into man and had to be dealt with at the Cross. Now Jesus Christ, exalted through us, will create a surge of revival and awakening that cannot be stopped.

In a West Coast city a few years ago, I bumped into a pastor friend with whom I'd gone to Bible school. We were overjoyed to see each other again and spent a couple of hours together, entertaining his son and associate minister with our old stories. He remembered things I'd long since forgotten—about the raw, unbridled power of God that had been loosed in our young lives as we'd thrown ourselves at the feet of Jesus in a humble desire to know Him. I suddenly realized his growing surprise at the stories I'd forgotten. With sadness, I finally understood that even with thirty years in the pulpit, he'd never again experienced the primitive power of the living God since those early days. *He thought living in the past was normal. I thought living in the present was.*

We were both wrong. *Dying is normal; then Jesus can take us beyond.*

Be With Jesus

Prayer is not merely talking to God. Prayer is fellowship, communion, and surrender to His lordship.

Prayer is not merely talking to God. Prayer is fellowship, communion, and surrender to His lordship.

Jesus taught the disciples to worship: "Our Father which art in heaven, hallowed be thy name" (see Matthew 6:9). The cherubs worship by saying, *"Kadosh, kadosh, kadosh,"* which means "holy, holy, holy." That's the kind of prayer God desires from us.

Worship is not two fast and two slow songs, with the chorus of the last one repeated four times. Today we often substitute singing for *true worship,* which is *simply exalting Jesus.* People too frequently worship their favorite singers instead of the Lord who created their voices.

"Thy kingdom come. Thy will be done." Christ, in essence, taught us to pray that *our* will would *not* be done, and that we would *not* establish our own kingdom on this earth (see Luke 11:1–4). This is a death-to-flesh prayer—surrender to Christ made possible by prayer alone. *This is God-wrestling prayer.*

God's goal is to raise up a people who have been with Jesus. The present-day ministry of Christ absolutely cannot be accomplished until we've been with Jesus. There is no way to enter the coming awakening without Spirit-to-spirit contact. No one is going to outlive Christ, and no one will live without Him. Without Him we won't live at all.

The mystery of spiritual intercourse with Christ is a fusion so powerful that when we leave that point of contact, spirit forces will know we've been with Jesus. This is the kind of deep intercession the church needs today, to go beyond the veil into the Holy of Holies and meet the King of Glory. *Being with Jesus is the key to world revival.*

At Pentecost, when Peter preached that "times of refreshing" would come from the Lord's presence (see Acts 3:20 NRSV), he meant that the outpouring of the Holy Spirit can only come from the presence of God. It cannot come from chasing a minister, a movement, a new experience, an anointing, or an attempt to do better. The strategic release of Spirit-to-spirit contact in the presence of the Lord will release a tremendous outpouring.

Peter understood that being with Christ means self dethroned, connection with the Spirit, and the very presence of the Lord bringing about a dynamic transformation. Some time after Peter's message at Pentecost, he and John walked into the city and saw a crippled beggar at the city gates. Peter said, *"Look on us"* (Acts 3:4).

Peter's realization was staggering: Peter knew the Christ who was crucified had risen, and that He was fully functioning and fully alive *in* him. Peter told the beggar to look upon him because the beggar would then see Someone other than Peter. The beggar saw the authority of a kingly Jesus, took Peter's hand, rose up from the ground, and ran into the temple, healed and shouting the praises of God! Nothing was special about Peter except that Peter had been with Jesus and become Christ's representation on the earth, fulfilling His present-day ministry.

This same Peter had been bound with fears, had run from Christ's trial, and had refused to acknowledge he even knew Jesus. But Peter had discovered the key to wrestling with God. Meeting Christ, Spirit to spirit, at Pentecost had a stronger impact on his life than knowing Christ face to face!

> *The most important thing to God today, for which He is ready to move heaven and earth, is manifesting His Son fully and completely in our lives.*

Don't forget: The most important thing to God today, for which He is ready to move heaven and earth, is manifesting His Son fully and completely in our lives.

Christ Has Appeared

After all the great outpourings of God's Spirit in the book of Acts, John wrote these beautiful words: "When he shall appear, we shall be like him; for we shall see him as he is" (1 John 3:2). For years ministers have presented this as a description of the afterlife, the Rapture, or the passage from this world to the next. But John means that when Christ appears, we shall be like Him. When will He appear? *It is not only referring to Jesus appearing at His return to the earth; it is as He appears right now—as His Spirit indwells us, we shall be like Him!*

Jesus knew that if He left earth and sent His Spirit, this "cloning process" in innumerable men and women would paralyze Satan. It did, for a season. The disciples not only took the city but the nation. Even the Roman Empire that persecuted them so ruthlessly became "Christian" after a period of time. *Satan cannot stop the astonishing manifestation of God's power when men, women, and children are fully immersed in Christ, and Christ is fully immersed in them.*

When Christ met Saul, Saul was temporarily blinded and

became an entirely different person. Paul didn't do that: it was Christ in him, the hope of glory. All Paul did was maintain Spirit-to-spirit contact with Jesus.

Christ can be seen today! Christ can be heard today! Christ can fully and visibly function in us, transcending our personality and agenda, causing the realms of darkness to tremble. Everywhere we go, Jesus softly speaks and His ministry continues. This is the great mission of the Holy Spirit. The Spirit's primary purpose is not to give gifts but to give us a revelation of Jesus.

Once, in prayer, Jesus gently promised He would open up Africa to me. He told me to go to a hotel in Mexico and pray with my wife. On the second day He told me to walk down the sidewalk, and, when a couple approached, to shake their hands, ask them to have lunch with us, and at lunch tell them there was a president in Africa they had met and that I would help. I did exactly what God told me. The couple turned out to be Maureen Reagan Revell, who had assisted her father, President Ronald Reagan, and her husband, Dennis; they had just come from meeting with various presidents of African countries. They were especially concerned about the new president of Uganda, who wanted to speak to broadcasters in America. Within seventy-two hours, Ben Armstrong, then president of the National Religious Broadcasters, officially confirmed that he would have the Ugandan president as one of the speakers at a conference in Washington, D.C. This African president rededicated his life to Christ, and he led two of the top leaders in his country to the Lord Jesus!

The person of the Holy Spirit connects us to the kingdom of God; this brings a transforming work in our lives, re-creating us in the measure of the stature of the fullness of Christ. Not just in spurts, but in His full blast of glory.

The mission of the Holy Spirit—unveiling the Holy of Holies, infusing us with the full manifestation of Jesus Christ—will cause the shadow of the weakest saint to heal the sick. *This power is only released when believers have been with Jesus.* No Old

Testament priest could survive the presence of God unless he entered the Holy of Holies focused single-mindedly upon God.

Prayer, this fusion with Christ, is indescribably precious to God; the Bible says He treasures the prayers of the saints. The apostle John saw, in the presence of Jesus, golden vials full of scent: the prayers of those who serve the Lord. The elders of heaven carried these vials and fell down before God's throne, worshiping God, acknowledging His power and glory and honor and blessing (see Revelation 5:7–10). This is the mystery of intimacy, the eternal consequence of all our prayers on earth. This is the mystery of wrestling with God.

We Settle for Tradition

During the writing of this book, I have been gutted by God. I have seen so much stinking, shameful flesh in my life, and I realize that for the greater part of my ministry, I myself have been on the throne of my life. The very movement I come from has some six-hundred million claiming the Pentecostal experience. Yet Pentecostalism has been packaged, perfumed, and promoted as if one gift of the Holy Spirit is going to raise the dead or usher in Christ's return. *God, forgive us for our arrogance.*

Jesus did not create Pentecostalism—we did. Pentecostalism is as bound by religious tradition as non-Pentecostalism. Out of our contentment at having "arrived," we develop a judgmental spirit toward those who do not operate in a certain gift of the Holy Spirit. When this happens, we are spiritually bound. Thank God for Pentecostal fire, but heaven help us if the fire goes out and we simply live off the smoke! There's nothing worse than a mean-spirited, holier-than-thou bragging about what we used to have and a condemning of those we perceive don't have what we had.

Young people and adults are bound by peer pressure, even in Christian circles, feeling they must exhibit certain outward manifestations, such as tongues or being slain in the Spirit; this kind of thinking casts in a false light the true work of the Spirit. In many cases, Pentecostalism is just another religious tradition. Speaking for myself, I know that before God, the flesh of a self-righteous, pharisaical Pentecostal stinks! Thank God for Pentecostal fire. When the fire goes out, and we strut our stuff, trying to live off the smoke, it's a sure indication Christ cannot manifest His glory in us or through us.

The cry of the Father's heart is that people everywhere might know Christ in the power of His resurrection. Yet we sell Pentecostalism to those wanting to "arrive," then wonder why, even with all this Holy Spirit power, the gates of hell prevail against the church. Why the high divorce rate (an increase of 800 percent since 1950, according to the *Charisma News Service*)? Why the addictions? Why do our young people leave the church? (Young people do not reject Christianity because the challenge is too demanding, they reject it because the challenge we present is too small.)

Jesus said, "You shall receive power, after that the Holy Ghost is come upon you: and ye shall be witnesses unto me" (Acts 1:8). How much power will we receive? Believers have no comprehension of the power that is yet to be released upon us!

This is much more than the baptism of the Holy Spirit. *Do we need the power of Pentecost?* Yes, all of it, and nothing else. All believers must be delivered from comfort zones to take part in the next awakening. When Christ's disciples gathered to pray in the Upper Room, the numbers decreased drastically. It was no party. There was no boasting and bragging about their successes and victories. None felt they had "arrived," even when the fire of Pentecost fell on them, because they still needed to be given to prayer. They surrendered their all, desiring Christ in all His glory.

How heartbreaking when we settle for tradition! We have been taught to experience Pentecost. *The habit is formed, but the hunger is lost.*

Our hunger for God is the greatest indication that the person of the Holy Spirit is on the throne of our lives. If we want to be with Jesus, we must be hungry for more than church. God is offended by neutrality. The fact is, we don't pursue prayer and passionately hunger for Jesus because of pride, unbelief, control, distrust, and the hoarding of our pulpit, ministry, kingdom, money, home, and church. Everything is "my, my, my—mine." If we walk in darkness, filled with anger, unforgiveness, self-righteousness, and envy, it's a sure sign we've not been with Jesus, Jesus has not been with us, and self is in control of our lives.

> *Our hunger for God is the greatest indication that the person of the Holy Spirit is on the throne of our lives.*

It is not what we do that defines who we are; it is who we are that defines what we do. If we say we have fellowship with Him and walk in darkness, we lie. We cannot abide in Christ unless we die to our desire to control and dominate in our flesh.

I was praying one day at the Mayflower Hotel in Washington, D.C., and the Holy Spirit told me to send a warning to Prime Minister Benjamin Netanyahu about a major distraction coming that day. His advisor kept asking what the distraction was. I told him I didn't know, but God said there would be one. Indeed there was. When Benjamin Netanyahu was pressed by President Clinton to relinquish territory, the Monica Lewinsky story broke in the middle of the meeting on national television.

Christ speaks! Christ works His purposes through believers who die to the flesh and come alive in Him.

Become the Army of God

Sincere Christian people can threaten the present-day ministry of Jesus Christ (see 1 Corinthians 3:1–3). We may do everything right as far as our own immediate circle is concerned, yet still be a million miles from the heart of God. We might even be famous with regard to the national or international Christian circuit, yet be blind to the person of Jesus Christ.

"Good" believers throw their entire lives into the temporal, only to face death with little of eternity in their portfolio. Only what stands up in the flames will pass through the portals of eternity. *Jesus did not come to make bad men good; He came to make dead men live.*

Good men might not see heaven, but dead men will inherit it. Isn't it amazing that one of the first statements out of the mouth of John, the Revelator, on the isle of Patmos, was that Jesus Christ is "the first begotten of the dead," and then when he saw Him, he fell at His feet as a dead man? Thank God that not only is He the first to come among the dead but *He is resurrecting men who are still alive, and the power of the Resurrection is killing their flesh.* They are dying to it, dethroning self, so they can rule and reign with Christ.

The Spirit of God is raising up an army of His servants who seek no temporal throne or temporal power, carry no carnal weapons of might, and do not stockpile the praises of men. Dead to themselves, their only hope is to be seated in heavenly places with Christ. They terrorize the demons of hell and torment principalities and powers because they cannot be bought by ambition. They alone will usher in the return of Jesus Christ.

These soldiers do not chase superstars of the faith to have their Bibles autographed, displaying how they *haven't* been with Jesus. They see only One, the Bright and Morning Star, Jesus, who has written His name on the tablets of their hearts. They lay their plans at His feet and embrace His plans for their lives. To them, fleshly pursuits are nothing more than a shunned eulogy. For them, the Holy Spirit is no longer imprisoned by flesh on the throne. In their wombs is the seed of God, coming alive to birth His destiny on earth. They are not simply burden-bearers for the high and mighty. They are warriors, commissioned by the Lion of Judah to gather the nations before Him. *They are the God-wrestlers.*

We can be part of this army of believers who will usher in the Second Coming. We will not be the most popular, nor should we seek popularity. Peter walked on the water to meet Jesus; later he realized that the One who walks in the midst of the storm cannot manifest himself with self in the way. Like Peter, Jesus calls us to walk with Him on the water, yet those left behind in the boat don't like water-walkers. Boat people go after God, then quickly retreat into familiar safe zones. They find it easier to surrender to the system than to be considered an outcast. Water-walkers have never been and never will be celebrated. Boat people get offended at God for not stilling all their storms, but *water-walkers realize that sometimes God stills the storms and other times He stills them in the midst of the storm.*

Christ in Us, Us in Christ

Man's greatest fear is to be rejected. Man's greatest desire is to be loved. We know we have been with Jesus when all self-consciousness leaves, the fear of man leaves, and the belief in our inferiority leaves. No one I've ever met felt more inferior than I did as a child.

We know we've seen the Lord when we lose the desire to please the world, to be vogue, fashionable, affirmed; when we know demons tremble as we pray; when we enter our prayer closets and can hardly believe the person we're hearing is actually us because of the boldness, the anointing, the glory, and the sensitivity. *If we surrender to the person of the Holy Spirit, and time is no longer an object, we've been with Jesus.*

God told me a door would open with *The Wall Street Journal.* Instead, I found myself being interviewed by Rabbi Lobovich in Crown Heights, sitting absolutely discouraged in an office that was knee-high in old newspapers. My cell phone rang, and a *Wall Street Journal* editor asked if I could have an article on Israel ready immediately for the Op-Ed section. The day it appeared, President Clinton was in New York to address the United Nations. I was told that not only had he read the article, but probably most of the world's leaders had. What an amazing God we serve. The inferiority of my background and lack of academic training didn't paralyze me. God said He'd created an opportunity with the *Journal;* dead to my flesh, I accepted His command and simply did what He said.

The union between Jesus and His bride produces life in the same way as intimacy between a man and a woman does. The gifts of the Spirit come not for spiritual entertainment, endorsements, or affirmations, but for the magnification of Jesus. *When we handle the Spirit's holy instruments with purity, we'll see Christ's ministry fulfilled in us.*

Moses came face to face with God. When the Lord said, "Fear not," Moses said, *"Hanai,"* which is Hebrew for "You see through me." Isaiah said the same thing. Being with Jesus requires transparency—God sees through us. Resistance is a stronghold Satan can use. The last thing the devil wants is Jesus to be seen through us. He doesn't fear us, but he does fear the face of Christ. Our flesh wants us to avoid exposing it, no matter what.

Christ desires to be with us, even though we're imperfect, but often we don't want to be with Him because we don't want Him to see us as we really are.

We've been taught to live up to a standard, and we're terrified to face the fact that we can't. So we play games to save face and come up with excuses for not living holy lives. The last thing we want is to be exposed as a failure, so in darkness we cover up or pretend. But when we walk in Christ's light, in the presence of God, we are exposed for what we truly are: frail human beings that can do nothing without Christ.

When we are free from the sense that God expects more than our capacity for holiness can provide, we can actually be free indeed, coming alive to the Spirit within us, waiting for us to step aside. God knows we're only dust. He understands we could never pull this off. That's why He grafted us into His Son. That's why He has given us access to His life. When we grasp this, we don't have to "play church" anymore. We're no longer troubled by the exposure of our weakness when we go to Him in prayer.

He always knew we were weak. Jesus didn't come to condemn us in our weakness; He came to be the strength that on our own we don't possess.

Christ Is Praying for You

Christ is praying for us even now: "He maketh intercession for the saints according to the will of God" (Romans 8:27). Why does Christ need to pray when He's in heaven? Why can't He just decree something from His throne? The intercession going on between Jesus and the Father is majestic and powerful. Christ is making intercession so His ministry will be released through us, which is the greatest threat to Satan's kingdom. Satan's greatest fear is a believer yielded to the holy fire of the living God, who manifests His glory from within.

Jesus' present-day ministry is no different than when He healed demoniacs, restored the withered hand, healed the impotent man, cleansed the leper, stilled the storm, restored sight to the blind, raised the dead, and fed the multitudes. He said, "He that believeth on me, the works I do shall he do also; and greater works than these shall he do; because I go unto my Father" (John 14:12). We will do greater works than Jesus because, in so many words, what is happening between Him and the Father will bring an even greater manifestation of His ministry on earth.

Jesus Christ is not listening to us and then repeating our prayers to the Father. He taught us to pray directly to the Father using His name, promising that it would be done. That power is already ours. Jesus is now praying for us to yield completely to His ministry and mission! If we don't, we are challenging Him for the lordship of our lives.

According to Ephesians, Christ today is praying that we will understand the full measure of His stature. He is praying for the kingdom of God to proliferate on earth. Jesus taught the disciples to pray, "Thy kingdom come. Thy will be done, as in heaven, so on earth" because this can and will come true before He comes a second time. Jesus is praying for the final harvest. He is praying for a blast of His glory to be unleashed. He is praying for a manifestation of himself within the common believer's life. He is praying for complete triumph over His enemies.

CHAPTER TWELVE

Beyond!

The Spirit and the Bride say, "Come."
REVELATION 22:17

Jesus planned a magnificent destiny for you, gave you incredible prayers and prophecies, unanswered until now. Step out to step up!

Have you been with Jesus? Are you a God-wrestler?

When we've been with Jesus, a consuming fire burns in our bones. Idols are cast down. Anything that takes the place of Christ's lordship is gone. Pride is broken. "The sacrifices of God are a broken spirit; a broken and contrite heart, O God, you will not despise" (Psalm 51:17 NIV).

Have you been with Jesus?

When we've been with Jesus, we've been sealed "unto the day of redemption" (Ephesians 4:30; see also Romans 3:24; 1 Corinthians 1:30), the redemptive work of Christ in the now! Jesus said,

"I go to prepare a place for you." This sounds like a mansion in heaven, but there is also another original Hebrew word, *makon,* that describes Christ as preparing for us a *position* (foundation, settled place). It's true we may have a mansion, but I believe we'll also have a position in the kingdom of God. We will rule and reign in the millennium *then,* but we rule and reign on earth *today.* When Jesus left this earth, He sent His Spirit to us, and then He sat down in heaven in intercession for us *now.*

Have you been with Jesus?

When we've been with Jesus, Christ's promises are ours! Jesus said to the Father,

> "The glory which thou gavest me I have given them; that they may be one, even as we are one: I in them, and thou in me, that they may be made perfect in one; and that the world may know that thou hast sent me, and hast loved them, as thou hast loved me" (John 17:22–23).

We know the glory the Father gave Jesus, and we have the closeness of being with Jesus. When Christ fully dwells in us, the world knows the Father has sent Jesus. What a way to live!

Have you been with Jesus?

Of the person who loves and obeys the Lord, Jesus proclaims, "We will come unto Him, and make our abode with Him" (John 14:23). By knowing, living, and breathing the fullness of being with Christ, and Christ being in us, we ask what we will and it shall be done. Jesus has all things under His feet; He is the Head of His body, Head over all things. This means, ultimately, that all things are under the feet of those who have been with Him.

Have you been with Jesus?

When we've been with Jesus, we no longer fear man. All signs of inferiority and self-consciousness are gone as Christ takes over. We rejoice in persecution and bless our enemies because our flesh is already dead, and our *all* is surrendered to His care. Our prayers frighten us, and making time for Him is no longer an object as our resources are given joyously back to the One through whom they came. Being with Jesus releases the gifts of the Holy Spirit, not to endorse a ministry or receive the approval of men but as a tool to accomplish His present-day ministry on earth.

Have you been with Jesus?

When we've been with Jesus, He makes known to us the mystery of His will, which is His good pleasure. The eyes of our hearts are flooded with light so we can know the greatness of His power. We live to the fullness of the measure of Christ, who makes all things complete and fills everything with himself (see Ephesians 1:9–23). We sit together with Him in heavenly places, and He demonstrates through us the riches of His grace (see Ephesians 2:6–7).

Have you been with Jesus?

When we've been with Jesus, we receive gifts to perfect and equip the saints, to build up Christ's body until we attain oneness in the faith and the comprehension of God's Son (see Ephesians 4:11–13). Our lives lovingly express truth and are no longer lived as the heathen with apathy, sensuality, greed, and every form of impurity.

Rush Through the Veil!

The veil in the Holy of Holies separated the glory of God, which represented His fullness, from the people. In Old Testament times, the high priest was allowed to enter the Holy of Holies only once each year. If he entered with impurity, he would die. He went to great lengths to become cleansed and purified from all sins—known and unknown. He would even stay up all night before he entered, so he could not become accidentally polluted through a dream and thus be unprepared by morning. Before he entered, the high priest would carefully tie a rope to his ankle. If he were struck down, the other priests could then drag out his body using the rope.

When Christ died, the veil in the temple was rent—supernaturally torn from top to bottom—opening up the Holy of Holies.

He did this *"by a new and living way, which he hath consecrated for us, through the veil, that is to say, his flesh"* (Hebrews 10:20). Today all are welcome to rush through the veil!

The flesh is man's best effort at a memorial, proving to God that "I, man, live righteously on this earth and can have authority and power without Christ's lordship." Knowing that the flesh represented everything foreign to the kingdom of God, Christ paid the supreme price of the flesh, making it possible for us, in Him, to step through the veil and have the same authority over our flesh that He has over His. Christ came in the flesh not only for our eternal salvation, but to provide access to enter into the glorious presence of the Father!

We need no longer try to be good and constantly fall short. There is a realm in glory where we can be seated—ruling and reigning with Christ in the now!

"Christ in you, the hope of glory" (Colossians 1:27) is not just a nice verse; it is a king's decree that only Jesus can live the Christ life through us.

Again, God is going to pour out power upon this generation more spectacularly than the world has ever seen. We are entering another book-of-Acts era, the final one. People will be lining up, hoping the shadow of humble, anonymous, praying God-wrestlers will pass by them and thus heal their sick bodies. Jesus will rule and reign, in full control. Once we realize that He alone has finished the work and conquered the flesh, we lay our flesh down day by day, hour by hour, and minute by minute so that Christ in all of His glory will be manifested through our lives.

When we have Christ and Christ has us—when Christ is fully revealed in us—we can enter the Holy of Holies and take authority over the flesh, and all His unanswered prayers will be fulfilled. *We can't have intimacy if we can't get through the door, and we can't get through the door if we're clinging to our sinful flesh.*

God can do little with us when we steadfastly retain self on the throne. *He can do anything with us when we die to self.*

The first time I met with Prime Minister Menachem Begin,

I had no invitation except by Jesus. One of the last times I met with him, several Israelis working at the Israeli Embassy in Washington, D.C., became infuriated with me because I believe in Jesus. They sent a secret communication, slandering me, to Prime Minister Begin. It was so malicious that a senior advisor sent me a mean-spirited wire saying never to come back to Israel. In prayer, the Holy Spirit told me exactly what had happened, who did it, what they said, and to whom. I flew to Washington and confronted them. They laughed and said, "But we're diplomats."

I said, "I am, too. I am an ambassador for Jesus Christ. God will [judge you] for slandering me and for trying to destroy my integrity with the prime minister."

"Go back to Texas," they said. "You're finished."

I did go back to Texas, but only to catch a flight to Jerusalem. I sent a wire to the senior advisor and the prime minister that I was coming to meet with them. The senior advisor was furious when I arrived, but I told him everything the Holy Spirit had said, and he was amazed: "I believe God has truly told you these things, because I thought that you were from Washington, D.C., as part of the intelligence secret service or something."

I said, "I'm in the Lord's service, and it's no secret."

He called the prime minister, who met with me. To my amazement, Menachem Begin said, "Would you host an official delegation for me to meet with when I come to America in a few weeks?"

We met him at the Waldorf Astoria in New York City along with the two men who had tried to destroy me. That's the meeting where the Spirit of God fell; Begin wept and said, "The only thing I can say is that the Spirit I sense in this room is the spirit of the redemption of Israel." Shortly thereafter, those Israeli diplomats were sent home.

"At destruction and famine, thou shalt laugh" (Job 5:22).

The Tabernacle in Us

"After this I will return, and will build again the tabernacle of David. . . . That the residue of men might seek after the Lord, and all the Gentiles, upon whom my name is called," saith the Lord, who doeth all these things. (Acts 15:16)

This prophetic word from the apostles reflects the prophecy given to Amos:

"In that day will I raise up the tabernacle of David that is fallen, and close up the breaches thereof; and I will raise up his ruins, and I will build it as in the days of old" (Amos 9:11).

These passages are talking about a latter-rain outpouring of the Holy Spirit, a heavenly visitation. The restoration of the tabernacle points to the restoration of the Holy of Holies and priests entering filled with the glory of God. These priests will come out of the Holy of Holies like Moses, with their faces shining with the reflection of and in complete oneness with the Lord, overflowing with His glory and love, filled with purpose. They'll realize the full mission of the Holy Spirit is not for personal entertainment but for divine destiny, to bring in the greatest global harvest in history. This mighty move will cause human personalities to be overshadowed and human programs to be abandoned because of the Lord's presence (see Acts 3:19). We are these priests!

There is no counterfeit to being with Jesus. Jonathan Edwards described a genuine revival of those who had been with Jesus in Northampton, Massachusetts, and neighboring towns and villages in Puritan Sage in 1735. He said,

As the number of true saints multiplied, the town seems to be full of the presence of God. It was a time of joy in families on account of salvation being brought unto them. . . . The spirit of God began to be so wonderfully poured out in a general way throughout the town, people had soon done with their old quarrels, backbiting and intermeddling with other men's matters.

This is a shadow of what we can expect.

The angels, day and night, worship God in His glory: *Kadosh, Kadosh, Kadosh*. This is the same glory Paul said will be restored. God is going to restore the glory of the priestly role; we, in word and deed, will become priests and kings unto God.

The word *glory* comes from another Hebrew word, *kabod,* which means "heavy, hanging down," referring to weightier matters, used in the context of marriage. The *hupah* (bridal canopy) at Jewish weddings is the symbol of this weightiness. There is a point at which Christ and His body will make supernatural, Spirit-to-spirit contact and will release God's *kabod* with all its heaviness, majesty, and might.

Remember Hosea saying that on the third day God will restore us to life in His presence? We are in the third day; a restoration of the tabernacle of David is taking place, allowing us to enter the Holy of Holies and live in intimacy with Christ. Entering the Holy of Holies, we truly live and have our being in Jesus.

The Obstacle to the Holy of Holies

The purity of God cannot dwell with the stench of flourishing flesh in the Holy of Holies. When we try to enter into that sacred place with Jesus Christ, our flesh can negate our access.

God will restore all the gifts of His Spirit when there is evidence enough to convict us of having been with Jesus, so get ready: The Lord will manifest not one gift but all of them, in us and through us. When we operate in His gifts, we can expect the unexpected!

Only the ego, the self, the flesh can keep us from entering the Holy of Holies or receiving the gifts of the Spirit. The gifts of the sacred Holy Spirit cannot abide with self in the same tabernacle.

To us, nothing is more foul than the smell of stinking, rotting flesh. We do everything possible to avoid it. In news stories of death-causing disasters, we see people covering their faces to protect themselves from the stench. To the world, the smell of dying flesh is despicable. To God, when our egos are laid upon the altar and engulfed by the fire of the Holy Spirit, it is the sweetest aroma, the most refreshing fragrance He knows.

When the fragrance of Christ is flowing through us, the enemy most assuredly comes to neutralize us by wiping off the odor of God's presence. Whenever Jesus comes down, the enemy comes out.

In John Bunyan's classic *Pilgrim's Progress,* Pilgrim moves ever closer to the Holy City by struggling to overcome his flesh, which naturally shies away from holiness of any kind. Only through holiness, the absence of flesh, can we overcome and defeat Satan. The enemy doesn't fall down, defeated and groaning, after three verses of a song and a mumbled prayer. Satan is wily, conniving, and relentless. His strategy is to focus Christians on fixing their flesh— pampering, pacifying, and placating it, pretending it's not as bad as what the Bible makes it out to be and that it can be reformed.

This cycle of flesh is a cycle of deception. We believe we can keep the flesh alive and give up only the sin. Again, a person's deeds are not the foundation of the problem; the flesh is the root, and the actions are the fruit.

In our misunderstanding, we have propagated a cycle of repenting, trying to be good, failing, repenting, trying to be good, and failing again. No wonder our young people quit! They don't want to fight a battle they can't win.

The battle being waged over flesh has high stakes—the very success of our Lord Jesus Christ. His success means Satan's total defeat. That Christ will succeed in raising up millions called by His name and endowed with His power is the greatest threat Satan has ever encountered.

Think of what we will do together!

Will We Enter?

There is no greater need today than for believers to know that they know that they know they have been with Jesus. To die to our flesh; to go beyond the veil into the Holy of Holies; to grab hold of the King of Glory and not let go. The Word says, "Whatsoever ye shall bind on earth shall be bound in heaven" (Matthew 18:18). There is power available to us when we release the flesh and walk into His presence.

> *There is no greater need today than for believers to know that they know that they know they have been with Jesus.*

What kind of impact would the church have if we died to our flesh and lived for Him? If we didn't spend so much time trying to keep Christians from backsliding and instead labored to bring in the lost?

Because we don't call for flesh to burn, smolder, and smoke on our altars, we provide a revolving door instead of entering through the veil into holiness. Masses of Christians wander like gypsies from church to church, dazed and traumatized, trying to find another fix where they can see or feel a glimpse of the glory of God, because they can't seem to obtain it on their own. They hope for a more powerful service or a more anointed pastor. *We search for a spiritual high that can only be lived through the low of death.*

Self-esteem feeds inferiority and is never attainable for a Christian until he esteems Christ above all—then he'll be bold as a lion. As long as I have *me* on my mind, I cannot have the mind of Christ.

When we enter the Holy of Holies and are touched by the penetrating ray of God's light, we will never again be the same. Once we've been with Jesus, we will be shattered, heartbroken, and burdened if His glory is not there. All we'll ask for is the manifest presence of the Lord in our place, where we can dwell in the shadow of El Shaddai. Just one penetrating revelation of the person of Jesus Christ will change our lives forever.

The moment Jesus, the Last Adam, died in His flesh, the veil to the Holy of Holies was split and the glory of God was released, creating a mighty earthquake. When we declare lordship for only one Person on the throne of our lives, we release the Holy Spirit to rend the veil of our flesh; signs and wonders follow. Those who are hungry for the presence of Jesus will step beyond the veil and allow the Holy Spirit to burn away the impurities of their flesh. *They will behold the Lamb of God and look to Jesus, faith's Author and Finisher.* The fear of God will come into their lives; smug, content Christianity will be a thing of the past.

When I first went to Israel in 1972, I met a businessman who showed our group a Babylonian art exhibition. I shook his hand and said, "Thank you so much, Joseph." He immediately called me into his office and asked why I called him Joseph. Embarrassed to have addressed this esteemed gentleman by his first name, I apologized. He said, "My name is Reuben. That's how I introduced myself, Reuben Hecht."

I apologized again, saying it was a mistake, but he insisted it was no mistake. He said his father, on his deathbed, had told him, "Israel will be born [as a nation], and you will feed Israel bread. And your name shall be Joseph." He had built the newly formed nation's granaries but had never changed his name. Reuben was convinced that God spoke through me because the Holy Spirit had revealed to me the name his father had given him. This was the beginning of an incredible friendship that lasted until Reuben's death. While he lived, he became a mentor in my life and my dearest friend in the nation of Israel. He was, without question, one of the most respected, venerable, and influential men in the nation, serving as senior advisor to two prime ministers and greatly influencing Israel's direction. We had many marvelous adventures together. I never had a finer friend than Reuben Hecht.

Shortly before he passed away, we stood one day on the top floor at Haifa University, looking out as we talked. I was almost moved to tears to know this might be our last conversation, and that I might never see him again, even in eternity. He knew I wanted him to receive Christ more than anything in the world at that moment.

"I can see the plains of Megiddo there, where it will all end," he said softly, pointing out the window. "And just behind me a few miles is Nazareth, where it all began."

Then he turned to me with a half smile and said, "I believe."

Oh, that men would praise the name of our wonderful and glorious Lord! The tears I'd held back streamed down my face as I hugged my beloved friend.

Come Through the Veil

Jesus wants us to come through the veil and be with Him, live with Him, breathe His very Spirit. In Him we live and move and have our being. He wants to order our steps so every fiery dart of the enemy will be deflected. He wants us walking in His blood trail so the demonic hoards of hell cannot sniff us out to destroy us.

It's time to expose the devil and allow the Holy Spirit to teach us about the King of our life—His behavior in us and our behavior in Him. When we go after Jesus, the enemy goes after us, because we have become a threat to his kingdom and his territory will be lost.

When we go after Jesus, the enemy goes after us, because we have become a threat to his kingdom and his territory will be lost.

It's time to admit that the Christ life manifested truly in us cannot be realized by mere religious tradition, no matter how sincere, until we acknowledge that we are in a state of rebellion against the King and are headed full speed away from Him. We will see clearly that religion has become integrated into our secular society and has been digested to the degree that the values the last generation held are disregarded as obsolete.

We must confess that our society has redefined, retarded, and repackaged our Christian values and filtered them back to the church, watered down, neutered, and lifeless—leaving Christians in a state of passivity, void of the desire to sacrifice and suffer for Christ, lacking holiness and passion. Substituting book-of-Acts faith for religious flattery, in God's eyes, is packaged poison: *Looks good externally but will kill you if you swallow it.* Without a holy fear of God burning in our bones, we are left with dull senses for the person of Jesus Christ and tone-deafness to the voice of the Holy Spirit.

God is waiting for you to part the veil and go beyond so the world will truly know you've been with Jesus! The Father is listening for the heartbeat of Christ in you. When He hears it, all heaven will be authorized to move on your behalf.

This is no time to be thinking about whether or not we have the person of the Holy Spirit. *There is only time to completely surrender the throne of our lives so the Holy Spirit has us.* A great awakening is coming. For those who are hungry and determined to be with Jesus, God will kiss them and move them from the natural. The unsaved will look at them and see the radiantly glowing face of an eternal Christ. More will be accomplished in one day by these saints than the average Christian will see accomplished in a lifetime. *These are the God-wrestlers.*

> The people that do know their God shall be strong, and do exploits. . . . They that be wise shall shine as the brightness of the firmament; and they that turn many to righteousness as the stars for ever and ever. . . .
>
> But thou, O Daniel, shut up the words, and seal the book, even to the time of the end: many shall run to and fro, and knowledge shall be increased. (Daniel 11:32; 12:3–4)

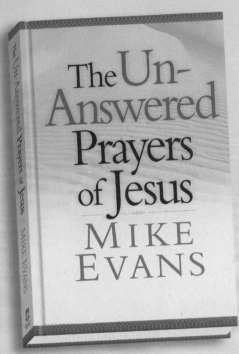

Jerusalem
PRAYER TEAM

"Pray for the peace of Jerusalem" Psalm 122:6

The Jerusalem Prayer Team is an intercessory movement to *"guard, protect, and defend Eretz Yisrael until the Redeemer comes to Zion."* This prayer movement was launched in June 2002 by Mike Evans. The Jerusalem Prayer Team established the goal of enlisting one million members to pray daily for the peace of Jerusalem according to Psalm 122:6.

The Jerusalem Prayer Team was birthed out of a one hundred year prayer meeting at the ten Boom home in Holland. It ended when the family was taken to the prison camps for saving 800 Jewish lives. Three hundred prominent American leaders such as Dr. Tim LaHaye, Rev. Jack Hayford, Dr. Pat Robertson, Mrs. Anne Graham Lotz, and thousands around the world are part of this prayer movement.

Be a part of prophecy today by joining. Membership is free. For more information, please visit our website at www.jpteam.org.

Name _____

Address _____

City _____ State _____ Zip _____

Email _____

Phone _____

Free gifts for new members.

Jerusalem Prayer Team • P. O. Box 210489 • Bedford, TX 76095 • jpteam@sbcglobal.net